BIHU FESTIVALS

All-inclusive elucidations

DR PRADIP NEOG

INDIA • SINGAPORE • MALAYSIA

Notion Press

No. 8, 3rd Cross Street
CIT Colony, Mylapore
Chennai, Tamil Nadu – 600004

First Published by Notion Press 2021
Copyright © Dr Pradip Neog 2021
All Rights Reserved.

ISBN 978-1-63745-493-0

CONTENTS

Contents

PREFACE

Why this Book?

Assamese people have been celebrating three Bihu festivals since pre-historic period at three different stages of Sali-paddy cultivation. They are called as Bohag Bihu, Kati Bihu and Magh Bihu. The intangible traditional heritages related to the Bihu festivals are outstandingly enormous and superlative. Varieties of productive rituals, superbly alluring dance forms, enthralling music, fabulous songs, prototypical musical instruments, games and traditional musical programmes are integral part of celebrating these festivals.

The need and scope of writing an all-inclusive book on the Bihu festivals in English language have been perceived from several perspectives:

The very word Bihu is recognized as cultural identity of Assamese people. The Bihu festivals, Bihunach (Bihu-dance) and Bihunam (Bihu-songs) are breathtakingly dear to all the Assamese people. Every Assamese is ardently proud of the rich heritages of the Bihu festivals, and enthused to celebrate, promote, preserve and safeguard those. Therefore, every Assamese ought to know about the wonderful intangible traditional heritages of the Bihu festivals thoroughly so as to celebrate satisfactorily, be proud genuinely, promote dynamically and to take responsibility of preserving and safeguarding.

There is no dearth of literature in Assamese language to know about the Bihu festivals. Several dozens of books and several hundreds of articles have been published in Assamese language on various aspects of the Bihu festivals. However, no book has so far written in English language which presents all-inclusive elucidations. Nevertheless, at present considerable numbers of Assamese people particularly, the youngsters are relatively more familiar to read various stuff in English language. The main target readers of this book are thus the Assamese people who are more familiar in reading in English language.

The second perspective of writing this book is that it would serve as an authentic resource book for revealing the valuable archetypical intangible cultural heritages of Bihu festivals as well as Assamese culture to the world. It might particularly be useful to obtaining global and national recognition of Bohag Bihu. Recently, on 20th September, 2020 the North-east Zone of the International Council on Monuments and Sites (ICOMOS) of UNESCO organised a Webinar on Bohag Bihu with the ultimate objective of enlisting Bohag Bihu as UNESCO's intangible cultural heritage. The author was one of the invited panellists in the Webinar and presented distinctive features of Bihunach and Bihunam. Later, ICOMOS uploaded an elaborate version of my lecture in the form of an articles entitled as 'Glorious intangible resources of Bihu festivals' has been uploaded in the website of 'International Committee on Intangible Cultural Heritage'(ICICH). This rich experience has further strengthened my conviction regarding scope and relevance of the book as valuable resource to be utilized for the purpose. The said experience also inspired me to expand and customise contents of couples of chapters so that the book better serves the purpose.

The book would also be advantageous to utilize for the authors and journalists to write articles on any subject-matter of Bihu-culture illustratively, accurately and authentically. Furthermore, quite obviously, this book would serve as a resource book in carrying out researches on Bihu festivals, Bihu-culture and Assamese culture as a whole.

Utmost care has been taken to present all the contents correctly and logically based on athetic sources, extensive study and research, and personal experiences. Even so, possibility of unintentional errors cannot be nullified in writing this book. The intangible cultural heritages of the Bihu festivals are enormous, exceedingly diverse, categorically archetypal and subjected to variation according ethnic groups, communities and localities. So, there could be unintentional omission and commission. Readers may kindly inform undersigned for any such mistake, so as to make correction in next edition.

Hope the book will contribute well towards popularising, disseminating, safeguarding and preserving the wonderful intangible cultural heritages of the Bihu festivals. At this juncture, I would like to cite this quote of Mahatma Gandhi: *"Satisfaction lies in the effort, not in the attainment, full effort is full victory"*.

Jorhat, the 5th January, 2021   **Dr. Pradip Neog**
pradipkneog@gmail.com
91-9678003670

ACKNOWLEDGEMENTS

I have inspired to write this book primarily because of the outstanding magnitude of the three Bihu festivals with regard to varieties of prototypical intangible cultural resources. These resources have been developed as a result of the contributions of innumerable traditional artists and intellects across many centuries. So, my foremost gratitude goes to all those anonymous artists and intellects.

Many books and articles have been written in Assamese language by many authors on various subject-matters of the Bihu festivals. Many of those contributions helped me directly or indirectly in writing this book. Several kinds of documentations in the forms of audio and video also facilitated me in the project. I therefore, sincerely express gratitude to all those authors and contributors.

My father, Late Ghana Kanta Neog and mother Late Mohita Neog were progressive, broad minded and caring enough for which I could not only get good education and all-round nourishments but also could participate in Hunchari of Bohag Bihu in my village during my childhood. The experience I gained by participating in Hunchari, and watching Jeng Bihu in my village has been serving as valuable groundwork in all my works on Bihu-culture. Moreover, nothing significant in my life would have been possible without their care, support and blessings. I am obviously ever grateful to them. I am also thankful to those with whom I gained the rich experience.

My father in law Padma Shri Dr. Laksmi Nandan Bora and mother in law Srijuta Madhuri Bora have always been inspiring me to carryout literary and cultural works to the best. Being a highly acclaimed eminent author of Assamese literature, the library of my father in law is outstandingly enriched with valuable books, and I could easily use several books from his library in the process of writing this book. For all these, I express deep sense of gratitude to both these most honourable relatives of my life.

The generous support, unconditional sacrifices and deep love of my beloved wife Dr. Seuji Bora Neog are invaluable in life. She has always been encouraging and supporting generously in all my projects. I therefore take this opportunity to offer heartfelt thanks and love to her. My thanks also go to my children Prerona and Prateek for their encouragements, and also for their confidence on me.

Dr. Sajib Borua one of my professional colleagues and a sincere social activist has been supporting me in my literary and cultural works for decades. Being an earnest scholar of Bihu festivals and experienced organiser of Bihutoli, he provided me several valuable facts and ideas for this book along with regular encouragement. I take this opportunity to express my heartfelt thankfulness to him for all his supports.

Pabitra Mohan Phukan, secretary general of 'Bihu Surashya Sommitty, Assam' has been putting untiring efforts for several decades for safeguarding, protecting and spreading of the traditional intangible heritages of the Bihu festivals. He generously extended hands to me in this project by providing several significant facts and photographs. So, I sincerely express my heartfelt thanks to him.

Bimala Gogoi Gohain, a veteran Bihuwati and social activists, and her daughter Kabyashree Gohain have provided several important resources for this book. I express heartily thankfulness to both of them.

Several experts and social activists in the field of Bihu festivals offered good wishes and inspiration to take up and complete this project. I express gratitude to all of them. Several photographs included in the book have taken from various websites. I express thankfulness to all the contributors of the photographs.

Late Maghiram Bora of Jorhat was co-investigator of my first research project on Bihu festivals which was carried out in early part of eighties of 20th century. I could substantially upgrade my knowledge and experience on Bihu festivals from him, and hence, it is my duty to express deep sense of thankfulness to him for all my works in this field.

Kishore Saikia, a promising artist in the field of canvas art and clay modelling has contributed in the book with two art pictures. Kashmiri Hazarika, Dipanjali Saikia, Madhusmita Dutta, Joydeep Dutta, Jamini Khonikar and several others provided generous support and help of various kinds. So, my thankfulness flows to all of them them.

I am also thankful to the team of Notion Press, for shouldering the responsibilities of designing, publishing and marketing the book.

Above all, I offer profound gratitude from my soul to the Almighty for blessing me to take up and complete this project.

Jorhat, the 5th January, 2021

Dr. Pradip Neog
pradipkneog@gmail.com
91-9678003670

Chapter I

AN OVERVIEW OF BIHU FESTIVALS

The Assamese people celebrate mainly 3 agrarian traditional festivals in 3 different stages of cultivation of Kharif-paddy or Sali-paddy, the main crop of the state. These three festivals are – Bohag Bihu, Kati Bihu and Magh Bihu. The festivals befall in 3 different seasons of a year: Bohag Bihu in the spring season, Kati Bihu in autumn and Magh Bihu in winter season.

The intangible heritages of the Bihu festivals including rituals, music, dance, games, traditional cuisines, typical snacks, and festivities are superbly extensive and wide-ranging. Traditionally, more than 40 kinds of rituals are performed systematically in the three Bihu festivals. These rituals not only reflect the religious faiths and actions of Assamese people, but also their rich culture, indigenous technical knowledge (ITKs), philosophies and occupational acumens. Majority of the rituals are productive in modern era too. The most alluring and attractive intangible heritage of Bohag Bihu are its distinctive dance form, songs and music. The dance form is called as Bihunach, the archetypical songs are called as Bihunam or Bihugeet, and the typical musical instruments are called as Bihubadhya.

This chapter aims at introducing all the major components and intangible resources of the Bihu festivals so that a reader even being unfamiliar to these festivals can gain understanding on the festivals in abridged form. In other sense, abstracts of all the chapters of the book are presented in this chapter in nutshell. Thus, this chapter can be regarded as introduction of book.

Bihu as identity of Assamese People

Bihunach, Bihunam and Bihu festivals are breathtakingly dear to the Assamese people. Majority of Assamese people can sing Bihunam and perform Bihunach. Whenever an Assamese expresses joy in any occasion spontaneously, she or he dances Bihunach and/ or sings Bihunam – no matter whatever the occasion and reason of celebration. Assamese people spontaneously perform Bihunach and/ or sings Bihunam in winning games and sports, in doing good result in education, in achieving bumper harvest, in getting any good news and the like. When such a celebration occurs in group, the magnitude of dancing Bihunach and singing Bihunam becomes more fabulous.

Moreover, Bihunach, Bihunam and Bihu festivals are recognized as cultural identity of Assamese people. In fact, the very word Bihu is considered as the cultural identity of Assamese race. Every Assamese is highly proud of the awesome prototypical cultural resources of the Bihu festivals. It is opined or said that - Bihunam and Bihunach are in the blood of Assamese people - Bihu is in the breathe of Assamese people –Bihu is dearest of the dearest– Bihu is heart of Assamese people – Bihu will be there till Assamese race exists – Assamese race will be there till Bihu exist. The legendary Assamese singer Dr. Bhupen Hazarika expressed in one of his evergreen songs that Bohag Bihu is the life-line of Assamese race.

Overview of Bohag Bihu

Bohag Bihu is celebrated prior to initiation of the activities of *Sali*-paddy cultivation. It starts on the last day of the month of Cho't of Assamese calendar. The date usually befalls either on 13th or 14th April in Gregorian calendar. It is celebrated for 7 days. As said earlier, among the three Bihu festivals, Bohag Bihu is the most extensive, joyful and colourful in terms of rituals, dance, songs, music, cultural functions, and days of celebration. Moreover, it is celebrated for more days as compared to that of other two Bihu festivals. Bohag Bihu is also regarded as New Year festival, as because the Assamese New-year begins on first day of the month of Bohag. The day of commencing Bohag Bihu also bears significance as Vishuva Sankranti.

The inherent purpose of celebrating Bohag Bihu is to worship to God(s) for exclusive growth of *Sali*-paddy leading to bumper harvest.

Another purpose is exchanging love, affection, gift etc. and rejoicing the wonderful spring season and traditional festivities. Moreover, the obvious purpose of the festival is to gain all-round wellbeing and prosperity of self, family and society by obtaining blessings of Almighty and respected ones.

Overview of rituals of Bohag Bihu

The rituals performed in Bohag Bihu are substantially more as compared to that of Magh Bihu and Kati Bihu. There are rituals reassuring to all the said purposes of the festival, and these are performed systematically for seven days. Each of the seven days has specific name and specific mandatory rituals are performed in each day. The seven days together is called as Xaat Bihu - means seven Bihu of seven days. The names of these seven days are – Goru Bihu, Manuh Bihu, Kutum Bihu, Haat Bihu, Tantar Bihu, Nangal Bihu and Chera Bihu. Of course there are a few variations in naming the seven days among localities as well as communities which are discussed in another chapter. A few most archetypical rituals of Bohag Bihu are as hereunder:

> ➤ Washing and caring bullocks and cows.

> ➤ Feasting explicit traditional cuisines of medicinal value.

> ➤ Eating selected bitter nourishments at empty stomach.

> ➤ Taking bath by applying traditionally prepared paste of medicinal value.

> ➤ Cleaning agricultural implements.

> ➤ Cleaning weaving implements

> ➤ Keeping auspicious items at roofs of house and cattle-shed

> ➤ Visiting parents by married daughter.

Overview of Traditional Games of Bohag Bihu

Two interesting and prototypical traditional games namely Koni-yunj (egg fighting) and Cowry-khel are organised as part of celebrating the festival in which menfolk take part with immense enthusiasm. (Photographs of selected rituals and games of Bohag Bihu are placed in Appendix I)

Classic gifts in Bohag Bihu

Bihuwan and Kopouphul (Rhynchostylis) bear special significance in Bohag Bihu. Bihuwan is a specially woven prototypical scarf or towel like item of Assamese culture. The females present Bihuwan to dear ones and respected ones as special gift at the occasion of Bohag Bihu. Assamese women start weaving Bihuwan well ahead of Bohag Bihu so as to present in the festival. Gamosa is another name of the same item, and is used by Assamese people for various purposes, particularly as towel and also as muffler. At present it is also used to felicitate personalities in meetings etc. It is so archetypal that currently some people use it as a kind of symbolic piece of costume to depict identity as Axomiya (Assamese people). The process of obtaining Geographical Indications (GIs) for Gamosa as a prototypical resource of Assamese culture is in progress. The word Axomiya refers to Assamese people and also Assamese language.

Kopouphul, the majestic and appealing orchid with big inflorescences blooms at the time of Bohag Bihu. Gift of Kopouphul from boyfriend or husband at the occasion of Bohag Bihu is regarded as especial by an Assamese girl or woman. The English name of Kopouphul is Fox tail orchid (Rhynchostylis).

Overview of Dance and Songs of Bohag Bihu

The most alluring, attractive and prototypical intangible heritage of Bohag Bihu are Bihunach and Bihunam. Bihunach is superbly appealing folk dance with typical rhythms, typical movements, typical twisting of waist, typical gyrating, typical poses, typical expressions.

Bihunam are also superbly fabulous and distinctively archetypical traditional songs of Assamese culture. They are distinctive and of high standard not only with regard to lyrical attributes but also in term of rhythms, tunes and ways of singing. Moreover, the magnitude of Bihunam is incomparably enormous. Several thousands of Bihunam have so far been composed across many centuries out of which more than 5000 have been documented in printed form in modern era. The subject-matters of Bihunam are also exceedingly diverse. There are Bihunam on all aspects related to Assamese agrarian life. Love is at the core of majority of the Bihunam. More than hundred tunes of singing Bihunam have become evergreen and established as prototypical as a result of singing Bihunam in many villages every year over centuries.

Total seven numbers of musical instruments are recognised as Bihubadya. They are - Bihu-dhol, Mohor-xingor-penpa, Toka (Mati-toka and Haat-toka), Gogona and Xutuli, Pati-tal and Baanhi. Out of these, the first five are prototypical and made of locally available materials. (Photographs of Bihubadya are placed at Appendix VII)

Overview of Rati Bihu and Jeng Bihu

Rati Bihu and Jeng Bihu were two fabulous programmes held in midst of nature as part of celebration of Bohag Bihu. It is postulated that that these programmes were held since pre-historic period. However, at present these programme are not held in midst of nature due to changed socio-cultural, educational and occupational scenario. Of course, both are showcased in cultural functions organised at the occasion of Bohag Bihu. Both Rati Bihu and Jeng Bihu were also called as Gostolor Bihu, Bonor Bihu and Maiki Bihu. Moreover, Jeng Bihu was also called as Toka Bihu, Gabhoru Bihu, and Senehi Bihu

Rati Bihu was held in night in forest. A group of grown-up girls and a group of grown-up boys participated by maintaining decent distance in Rati Bihu. The group of girls performed Bihunach, sang Bihunam and played Toka, Gogona and Xutuli. The group of boys sang Bihunam and played mainly Mohor-xingor-penpa. Additionally, in a few villages Bihu-dhol and Pati-tal were also played by the group of boys in Rati Bihu. (Picture of Rati Bihu and Jeng Bihu are placed at Appendix IV)

Jeng Bihu was also held in midst of nature but at daytime, and a group of grown up girls performed Bihunach, sang Bihunam and played Toka, Gogona and Xutuli. There was no participation of menfolk in Jeng Bihu. The Assamese world Jeng means branch of Bamboo tree. In some localities Jeng was placed around the spot at which girls danced, and so, the name Jeng Bihu. In present era this name has become more popular, and hence it is used in this book to mean the programme. The spot at which girls performed Bihunach in Rati Bihu or Jeng Bihu was called as Bihukhola.

Overview of Hunchari

Hunchari is the most illustrative and reverential among three traditional programmes in which Bihunach and Bihunam are performed by playing Bihubadya. The group which perform Hunchari is called as Hunchari-dal. Generally one Hunchari-dal is organised per village, and it performs Hunchari in courtyards of the families of the village by following several definite traditional norms. There are broadly four parts or components of Huncahari:

- ➤ Mangaldhani
- ➤ Hunchari–diha
- ➤ Bihu
- ➤ Ashirbad.

In the Mangaldhani and Ashirbad parts the Hunchari-dal blesses the family. In Hunchari–diha, and Bihu parts the Hunchari-dal sings Bihunam and performs Bihunach by playing Bihubadhya. Hunchari-diha is also called as Hunchari-ghokha.

Originally only menfolk participated in Hunchari. Later, another format has been evolved in which girls also participate. About evolution of this format is presented in another chapter. Hunchari was held in courtyards of families in many villages till the end of 20th century. Then onward it dwindled. At present, Hunchari is held in courtyard of families only in a few villages. However, it is showcased in most of the cultural functions organised in present era at the occasion of Bohag Bihu. (Photographs of Hunchari are placed at Appendix V)

Overview of cultural functions of Bohag Bihu

In present era, as part celebrating Bohag Bihu, cultural functions are organised in hundreds of places in the state throughout the month of Bohag. Assamese people living in outside Assam and abroad also organise such functions in celebrating Bohag Bihu. In such a cultural function, Hunchari, Rati Bihu and Jeng Bihu are performed as well as showcased, and exclusive programme on Bihunach is also held. Competitions of those are also organised. Moreover, programmes of celebrity artists on modern Assamese songs and modern Bihugeet are held extensively. Folk dance and folk music of various ethnic groups of Assam are also showcased.

Furthermore, at present programmes of Bihunach and Bihunam are also showcased in national and international cultural events. Such performances have already earned remarkable applauds wherever showcased. Several groups have bag prizes in competitions of folk dance organized in different parts of the globe. Musical performance of Bihubadya has also exceled in such events.

Even so, there is need and scope of showcasing the wonderful traditional dance form, songs and music of Bohag Bihu more extensively to the world.

Pitha and Jalpan of Bihu festivals

Preparation of varieties of traditional food items including especial cuisines, sweets and snacks is integral part of most of the agrarian traditional festivals. Varieties of traditional foodstuff such as Pitha, Laru, traditional refreshments called as Jalpan, and especial cuisines are prepared in Bohag Bihu and Magh Bihu. The Assamese word Pitha means flour. Pitha is typical cake or biscuit like confectionary items prepared from rice flour. Varieties of Pitha are prepared in both the Bihu festivals which include:

- ➢ Til-pitha
- ➢ Bor-pitha
- ➢ Chunga-pitha
- ➢ Ghila-pitha
- ➢ Tekeli-pitha
- ➢ Xutuli-pitha
- ➢ Joon-pitha
- ➢ Anguli-pitha
- ➢ Kandhuli-pitha
- ➢ Luthuri-pitha.

The different kinds of Laru are:

- ➢ Tilar-laru
- ➢ Narikalar-laru

- ➢ Sira-laru
- ➢ Pokamithoi
- ➢ Muri-laru

The traditional items prepared as Jalpan are:

- ➢ Sira
- ➢ Akhoi
- ➢ Hurum
- ➢ Handah
- ➢ Chunga-choul
- ➢ Komal-chaul
- ➢ Dua-bhoja.

In addition to the items mentioned above another sweet item called as Narikolar-sira is also prepared. Majority of the Pitha and Laru of Assamese culture are prepared with no or negligible amount oil. Furthermore, curd and molasses are arranged abundantly at the occasion of Bohag Bihu and Magh Bihu as because the items of Jalpan are preferably taken by adding curd and molasses. Selected varieties of rice are used in order to prepare different types of Pitha, and Jalpan. The word Choul means processed rice.

Overview of Magh Bihu

Magh Bihu is celebrated after harvesting of *Sali*-paddy. Thus it is a harvesting festival, and thanksgiving Almighty, community feast and rejoicing delicacies of varieties of traditional cuisines, Jalpan, Pitha, Laru are at the core. Hence, it is also called as Bhogali Bihu - festival of rejoicing delicacies of foodstuff. Bhogali means abounding with enjoyable foodstuff. It begins on last day of the month of Puh of

Assamese calendar and on 13th or 14th January according to Gregorian calendar. This very day also bears significance as Makar Sankranti. The last day of the month of Puh is called Uruka of Magh Bihu, and the first day of the month of Magh is called as Magh Bihu. The festival is celebrated for 2 to 5 days.

Basically, there are four purposes associated with celebration of Magh Bihu. Firstly, thanksgiving God(s) for obtaining harvest of *Sali*-paddy. Secondly, praying God(s) to gain blessings for prosperity of self, family and society. Thirdly rejoicing harvest, and feasting of varieties of traditional delicacies at community and family levels. Fourthly, relinquishing lassitude caused by pinching winter season so as to regain zest for efficient involvement in livelihood activities in coming days. The most distinctive rituals and festivities of Magh Bihu are as follows:

- Community feast

- Rejoicing warmth of Mezi (a prototypical bone fire of Assamese culture).

- Enjoying the night of Uruka in Bhelaghar(a prototypical makeshift cottage of Assamese culture).

- Rejoicing delicacies of several kinds of typical potato.

- Feasting varieties of Pitha, Laru, Jalpan, and traditional cuisines.

- Inviting friends and relatives and feasting together.

- Moh-yunj (Buffalo-fighting).

- Playing traditional games.

The Community feast of Magh Bihu is organised in the evening of the day of Uruka, and burning of Mezi is held at the dawn of first day of the month of Magh. A temporary tent called as Bhelaghar is prepared by using bamboo and paddy straw near the Mezi in which young menfolk stay in the night of Uruka and enjoy together by singing traditional songs and making fun. The community feast and Mezi are regarded as auspicious events, and organised by following definite rituals. The warmth of Mezi is believed as spirited for the whole year.

Preparation, feasting and sharing of various Pitha, Laru, Jalpan and traditional cuisines are more in Magh Bihu as compared to that of Bohag Bihu and Kati Bihu. All different Pitha, Laru, and Jalpan mentioned in case of Bohag Bihu are also prepared in Magh Bihu, and rather more abundantly. In addition to those, various traditional cuisines including of the typical species of potato are prepared and enjoyed. Inviting friends and relatives, and sharing the traditional foodstuff is customary in Magh Bihu. Assamese women start preparation of the traditional Pitha, Laru and Jalpan well ahead of commencing Magh Bihu festival. (Photographs of selected rituals and games of Magh Bihu and Kati Bihu are placed at Appendix II)

Overview of Kati Bihu

Kati Bihu is celebrated after about a month of panicle initiation of *Sali*-paddy crop. It is of one day duration festival and held on last day of the month of Ahin of Assamese calendar. This day is also significant as Kartik Sankranti. As per Gregorian calendar, the festival befalls in the mid of October.

The main purpose associated with Kati Bihu is protecting *Sali*-paddy crop from various pests, diseases, and other evils so as to obtain good harvest. Another purpose is praying God(s) for crop health and prosperity of family and society. A couple of rituals relating to both the purposes are performed with spiritual spirit.

The ritual performed relating to the first purpose is putting oil based lamps called as Chaki in *Sali*-paddy field, and worshiping

God(s) to protect the crop. The flames of the lamps evidently control many pests of crop. Pests are attracted by the flames of the lamps and thus get killed. In some villages, families put the lamps during the whole month of Kati starting from the day of Kati Bihu.

The ritual with another purpose is performed at family levels in homes. Every family puts oil-based lamps in front of courtyard and in front of a basil plant, and worships God(s) for prosperity and safety of family. As said earlier, the entertaining and feasting element in Kati Bihu is negligible, and therefore it is also called as Kangali Bihu too. Of course, one or two kinds of Pitha and Laru are prepared at the occasion of the festival.

Common Rituals of 3 Bihu festivals

1. Before a day or more of commencing any of the three Bihu festivals, every family carries out pre-festival cleanliness – cleaning of house, cattle shed, homestead and utensils. Traditionally cow-dung is used to clean floor and walls of the *katcha* houses.

2. Ploughing and digging of land are prohibited on the day of commencing any of the Bihu festivals. In case of Bohag Bihu and Magh Bihu this ritual is observed for first two days.

3. Community prayer is organised as part of celebrating all the three Bihu festivals.

4. Every family do especial prayer before taking breakfast on the day of any of the Bihu festivals.

5. Lunch is skipped on the day of any of the Bihu festivals.

Brief about origin of Bihu festivals

As postulated by majority of the researchers, Bihu festivals are about 5000 years old, and were initiated by Austroasiatic people who were the earliest inhabitant of Assam. They lived in the land of Assam during 3000 BC to 1000 BC. During 1000 BC various groups of Tibeto-Burman people came to Assam, and as a consequence of their immigration Austroasiatic people migrated to Meghalaya and Bangladesh. Of course, according to a few researchers Bihu festivals were initiated by Tibeto-Burman, and according couple of others by Tai-Ahom. A few others researchers postulated that Bihu festivals may be started as Vedic ritual.

At present, people of Assam are multi-ethnic, multi-linguistic and multi-religious. The major ethnic groups include Tibeto-Burman, Indo-Aryan, Tai-Ahom, Kuki-chin, Dravidian, Yogi, Tea garden labourers, Muslim and Bengali. Majority of these ethnic groups at present celebrate the Bihu festivals particularly, Bohag Bihu as the main festival of Assamese race. Thus, the Bihu festivals are by and large influenced by the cultures of all these ethnic groups. Of course, basically the intangible resources of the Bihu festivals are mainly originated from various ethnic groups of Tibeto-Burman, Tai-Ahom, and the Austroasiatic people. The major Tibeto-Burman ethnic people at present living in Assam include, Bodo, Chutia, Deuri, Dimasa, Garo, Hajong, Karbi, Mesh, Mising, Rabha, Thengal Kachari, Sonowal Kachari, Soronia Kachari and Tiwa.

Main Challenges towards Preservation of Bihu-culture

As a consequence of modernisation in present era, the traditional festivals and their constituents including rituals, folklores and folk dance have been losing original nature, and facing tremendous threat of existence all over the world. It is also occurring in case of Bihu festivals rather more intensely and extensively.

Majority of cultural functions organised in hundred places in the state as part of celebrating Bohag Bihu are primarily promoting modern and modern songs of celebrity artists which are presented with western musical instruments. Thus, these functions are rewarding only for the artists of modern music. At present majority of the said functions are organised with budget of more than 10 lakh but roughly less than 20 per cent of the budget is spent on programmes or activities which can promote traditional Bihunach, Bihunam and Bihubadya, and which can reward folk-artists reasonably.

Moreover, several worth adopting rituals of the Bihu festivals are in the process of becoming obsolete. Seems in the modern era, many of the young Assamese people possess insufficient knowledge and experience in order to practice, appreciate and promote the traditional resources of the Bihu festivals including the rituals, games and traditional forms of Bihunam, Bihunach and the Bihubadhya.

Social activists, researchers, authors and social organisations have been putting concerted effort towards safeguarding, preservation, education and spread of the intangible heritages of Bihu festivals. However, support of local government and national and international organisations is well felt to boost up such efforts. In this context, Nicholas Kotsiras, a political leader of Turkey said, "protecting ones culture does not happen by osmosis or by accident, as it requires the will of the individual as well as the support of the government and civil society to do so within an evolving multicultural society, focusing particularly on governmental support." He asserted it in his key note address delivered in international forum on 'Preserving Culture and Heritage through generation' held at Turkey during May, 11-14, 2014.

Chapter II

SEASONAL FEATURES OF BIHU FESTIVALS

Celebration of any agrarian traditional festival is largely oriented on nature and agricultural scenario in addition to socio-cultural and religious attributes of the people. The various rituals and festivities of the three Bihu festivals are finely attuned to the three seasons in which they are celebrated. It is therefore advantageous to know about the nature of the land of Assam as a whole, and also the distinctive features of the three seasons of the Bihu festivals. This chapter briefly presents natural richness of Assam, and the relevant features of the three seasons and their influences on the festivals.

Natural beauty and richness of Assam

The nature of the state of Assam is outstandingly rich with several rainforests, hills, rivers, streams, *beels* (large marshy areas) and river valleys. The bio-diversity is stupendously opulent with wide range of flora-and fauna including varieties of trees, shrubs, herbs, mammals, reptiles, birds, insects etc.

The state receives plenty of rainfall. The annual average annual rainfall is 2500-3000 mm. The main rainy season exists during June to September, but the most parts of the state also receive substantial rain in other months too. Hence, not only the forests but also the hills of state are evergreen.

The mighty river the Brahmaputra which is ranked 6th by width and 15th by length in the world flows throughout state. The Brahmaputra valley and the valleys of its tributaries are highly fertile, immensely rich in water resources, and especially suitable for paddy cultivation. The foot hills are suitable for wet rice cultivation and high hills are suitable for direct seeded rice cultivation. In addition to *Sali*-paddy, farmers of the state have been cultivating *Ahu*-paddy and *Boro*-paddy extensively. Mustard, Sugarcane, Jute, Black-gram and Green-gram are the main field crops other than Paddy. Citrus, Banana, Pineapple, Areca-nut, Coconut, Mango, Litchi and Jackfruit are the main major fruits of the state while several kinds of minor fruits are available in nature in all parts of the state. Most of the vegetables grow easily and luxuriantly in the state. The nature of the state is also enormously rich with wide range of medicinal plants. Moreover, there are total 803 big tea gardens across the state.[1] Additionally there are more than thousand numbers of small tea gardens. Total area under tea gardens in Assam is 3,12,210 hactare.[2]

Thus, whole state including the river valleys and hills remains green throughout the year. Beauty of each tea garden is exceptionally eye-catching: The gorgeous ever green tea plantations are like fresh green carpets spread in hectares of plain areas and hilly slopes throughout the state are is pure enchantment. Furthermore, the state of Assam is surrounded mostly by the Himalayan mountain range. Thus, the beauty of blue hills is seen from most part of the state, and so, it is also called as land of green valley and blue hills.

Seasonal magnitude of Bohag Bihu

The spring season befalls in the state of Assam during Bohag Bihu. This season is called as Basanta Ritu in Assamese language, and recognised as Rituraj(best season). Basanta means spring, and Ritu means season. In this season, the nature throughout the state becomes most splendid, and thus transpires fantastic festive environment. The weather condition is also enjoyable in this season – neither too hot nor too cold. Pre-monsoon rain starts in the state around the festival, and generally gets heavy rainstorms. The very rainstorms occurred at the time of Bohag Bihu are called as Bordoisila.

During the season, the scenic beauty of the whole state becomes magical from all spectacles. All kinds of the plants including trees, shrubs and herbs get new leaves, and many of them blossom with beautiful flowers of various colours and shapes. Several rare and beautiful species of orchid also blossom in this season. Many of the flowers of the season bear finest fragrance, and thus make the air enchanting. The rich wild life in the rainforests and hills start gaining strength with abundance of fodder and prey for wild life. The green hills become greener and fabulously flamboyant with patches of flowers of various colours. Many species of migratory birds come to this part of the globe in this time, and people often spontaneously enjoy their melodious singing everywhere and at any time, right from early morning to late night. Furthermore, it is the breeding season of fishes, and numerous fishes of many varieties demonstrate their tempestuous behaviour in all different sources of water including rivers, streams, canals and all sorts of marshy land. It is the breeding season of the migratory birds too, and in fact, that is the very reason of their migration to the state during this season.

The Fox tail orchid (Rhynchostylis) called as Kopouphul in Assamese language bears special significance in Bohag Bihu. As said earlier, Kopouphul (Rhynchostylis), the superbly exquisite orchid of majestic inflorescences. It blooms at the time of Bohag Bihu in the nature of Assam. At present some of the Assamese families also growing it in their gardens. The Assamese womenfolk adorn hair with Kopouphul during the festival, and also while performing Bihunach. It is also considered as especial gift of lover by an Assamese girl or woman. Womenfolk also prefer to use two other kinds of flowers for adorning hair especially in Bohag Bihu. They are Wax flower (Chamelaucium uncinatum) called as Togor-phul in Assamese, and the Indian Rose Chestnut (Mesua ferrea) flower called as Nahor-phul. The word Phul means flower. Another flower people put especial importance in Bohag Bihu is Kewda (Pandanus odoratissimus) called as Keteki-phul in Assamese. This marvellously aromatic flower blooms in nature of Assam at the time of Bohag Bihu, and people collect its inflorescences for its awesome fragrance. Keteki-phul is also regarded as an especial gift by a girl or woman from loved ones at the occasion of the festival.

Two birds are notably associated with Bohag Bihu. They are Koel (Eudynamys) called as Kuli-sorai, and Hawk-cuckoo (Hierococcyx varius) called as Keteki-sorai in Assamese language. The word Sorai means birds. Both are migratory birds of Assam. The Kuli-sorai starts singing with melodious voice at the advent of Bohag Bihu and makes the environment fabulously enchanting. It is therefore said that Bohag Bihu comes with singing of Kuli-sorai. As it is breeding season, the male of Kuli-sorai sings to allure female ones and also to inform its position. Keteki-sorai starts singing after a few days of starting singing by Kuli-sorai. "The males are easily detected by their repeated calls but can be difficult to spot. The call is a loud screaming three-note call, repeated 5 or 6 times, rising in crescendo and ending abruptly. It is heard throughout the day and frequently during moonlit nights".[3]

Thus, the very season of celebrating Bohag Bihu is naturally festive and romantic to a great extent. The Assamese people therefore become spontaneously stimulated to dance, sing, and play, and to make romance. They make it more romantic and festive with the programmes of Bihunach and Bihunam on one hand, and with traditional games and varieties of rituals on the other. The illustrious Assamese author Hem Barua delineated the seasonal impact of Bohag Bihu in these words: "The month of Bahag (April), flaming leaves of trees, and creepers add a refulgent lustre to nature. Leaves quivering in spring-breeze announce the advent of spring. From a distance the music of drums, buffalo-horns and takas (made of split bamboo) waft across open fields, rivers, rivulets and streams. Men's heart and minds get overpowered with music. The soft lustre of wild orchids called kapauphuls adds to the beauty of girls locks ready for dance. Millions of stars shine in the mekhela (skirts) borders. The ink-black clouds gather in the sky and announce the oncoming monsoons. The sky becomes randiant with lightning flashes. The urge to procreate rages in nature, the impulse to create and be fruitful. Around this fact of nature, the primitive man weaves cycles of festivals. The Bahag Bihu is a fertility-festival".[4]

Seasonal magnitude of Magh-Bihu

The chilliness of winter season in Assam normally reaches its peak in the month of Puh, and the pinching cold starts diminishing from Magh Bihu onward. So, the warmth of Mezi is quite enjoyable at the dawn of the day of Magh Bihu. Moreover, during winter season, most of the food items become readily available in the agrarian families of the state. Availability of milk becomes highest during this period of the year. The ducks also become fatty by consuming newly harvested rice, and duck-meat becomes tastiest. Most of the vegetables also become abundant in this period. Several indigenous as well as special kinds of potato are harvested just before the festival, and people enjoy those with traditional preparations. Moreover, winter is the main season of harvesting fish from the natural water sources including rivers, streams and *beels*. In some places therefore community harvesting of fish from such water sources is organised either on the day of Uruka or day before Uruka. Thus, at the occasion of Magh Bihu the agrarian families can afford to contribute generously for luxurious community feast, and can prepare the delicacies of traditional cuisines and confectionaries most abundantly.

Seasonal features related to Kati Bihu

At the time of Kati Bihu the fields of *Sali*-paddy in Assam become superbly gorgeous and promising with the maturing panicles on the plants. So, the agrarian families become optimistic of getting good harvest on one hand and dubious on the other hand for any possible damage of the crop. Various pests become more in this stage of *Sali*-paddy to eat up the crop. The very purpose of celebrating Kati Bihu is therefore associated with protection of the crop from pests, diseases and other evils. The main ritual of putting earthen lamps in paddy field also bears significance of the stage of the crop. The lamps evidently control pests of paddy field to a great extent as put throughout a field by all families as mandatory ritual of the festival.

Chapter III

SIGNIFICANCES OF SANKRANTI IN BIHU FESTIVAL

Sankranti means transmigration of the Sun from one Rāshi to the next in the Rashi Chakra of Vedic Astrology. Hence, there are 12 Sankranti in a year. Each Sankranti is marked as the beginning of a month in the sidereal solar calendars followed in Andhra Pradesh, Karnataka, Maharashtra, Tamil Nadu, Kerala, Odisha, Punjab, and Gujarat. On the other hand, in the sidereal solar Bengali calendar and Assamese calendar, a Sankranti is marked as the end of each month and the day following as the beginning of a new month.[5] This word Sankranti is also spelled as Samkranti in some parts of India.

The three Bihu festivals are at present celebrated at three different Sankranti. There is dearth of factual information to ascertain since when Assamese people started celebrating the festival in accordance with the three Sankranti of Assamese calendar. It is obviously the result of the influence of Aryan culture.

If we accept the postulations that Bihu festivals have originated from Austroasiatic culture, then it can well be assumed conjectured that Assamese people started to celebrate these festivals in accordance with three Sankranti at later stage as a result of the influence of Aryan culture. This hypothesis is also valid even if we accept the postulation that origin of Bihu festivals is of Tibeto-Burman culture. The Assamese calendar counted from the regime of the king Kumar Bhashkar Barman. "The Assamese calendar (Assamese 'Bhāskarābda') is a Luni-solar calendar, followed in the Indian state of Assam. The New Year in the Assamese calendar is known as Prothom Bohag. The calendar is counted from the date of the ascension of Kumar Bhashkar Barman to the throne of Kamrup".[6] "Bhaskaravarman (600–650) of the Varman dynasty was perhaps the most illustrious of the monarchs of the ancient kingdom of Kamarupa".[7] Furthermore, in case of most of the agrarian festivals the day of starting celebration was traditionally decided every year by village bodies or village heads based on the agro-climatic, socio-cultural and other ancillary factors.

In course time, due to the changes of culture and integration of ethnic groups as bigger group as well as races, in case of many such festivals the system of celebrating in accordance with dates of calendar evolved. Even today, in case of some of the agrarian festivals of some ethnic groups, the system of deciding dates of every year exists.

However, as the three Bihu festivals are at present celebrated as per specific dates of Assamese calendar at occurrence of three different Sankranti, it is advantageous to know and take into consideration of the significance of these Sankranti while celebrating these festivals. This chapter briefly present the significances of each of the three Sankranti:

Significances of Mahavisuva Sankranti

Mahavisuva Sankranti is also called as Mesha Sankranti. On this day, the Sun enters the sidereal Aries or Mesha rashi. It marks the beginning of Solar calendar, and hence, the day is regarded as New Year in most of the state as well as races in India. After Mahavisuva Sankranti the Sun moves in the northern direction. Therefore, this day of first movement of the Sun towards north is regarded as New Year. All over the country this day is considered auspicious and is celebrated with social, cultural and religious performances. The festivals celebrated in other states of India at occasion of this Sankranti by considering it as auspicious day are:

- ➤ Pana Sankranti in Odisha

- ➤ Pohela Boishakh in West Bengal

- ➤ Vishnu in Kerela

- ➤ Puthandu in Tamil Nadu

- ➤ Vaisakhi in Punjab

- ➤ Bikhoti Festival of Uttrakhand

As delineated in templesinindiainfo.com - according to Bhabisya Purana, when Bhishma, the grandfather of Kauravas and the Pandavas was lay on Shara Sajya (the bed of arrows) he felt too thirsty on the day of Jalavisuva. There was no water nearby in the ravaged battle-field of Kurukshetra. Then, Arjuna inserted an arrow deep into the ground with his powerful bow, and resultantly, water immediately discharge out in a stream to quench the thirst of the dying Bhishma. Out of contentment and compassion Bhishma conferred to Yudhisthira: Those people who would offer cold water to thirsty people on this day would not only be free from all sins, but also the departed souls of their ancestors as well as the Gods in heaven would be pleased. This saying of the Purana is observed with great reverence and people all over the country offer sweet-water to thirsty people as a religious rite".[8]

Significance of Makar Sankranti

Makar Sankranti marks the transition of the Sun into Makara rashi on its celestial path. It also marks transition of the Sun for the six-month - Uttarayana period. Makar Sankranti is therefore also called as Uttarayana – the day on which the sun begins his northward journey.

Makar Sankranti is considered as most significant among the 12 different Sankranti from the Astrological as well as religious points of view. Festivals are therefore celebrated in different parts of India on Makar Sankranti with immense auspicious spirit as well as religious faith and great joy. The major festivals celebrated on Makar Sankranti in different parts in addition to Magh Bihu include the followings:

➤ Maghi in Punjab, Haryana, Himachal Pradesh and Delhi

➤ Thai Pongal in Tamil Nadu

➤ Makara Sankranti in Odisha, Maharashtra

➤ Haldi-kumkum in Maharashtra by women

- ➤ Uttarayan in Gujarat
- ➤ Magha Saaji in Himachal Pradesh
- ➤ Maghe Sankranti in Nepal
- ➤ Khichdi Sankranti in Uttar Pradesh Bihar and Jharkhand
- ➤ Poush Sankranti in West Bengal
- ➤ Pedda Pandaga in Andhra Pradesh
- ➤ Sankrat in the Rajasthan
- ➤ Ghughutia or Kale Kauva in Uttarakhand
- ➤ Magey Sakrati in Himalayan regions
- ➤ Suggi in Karnataka

There are several reciprocally assuring interpretations and saying regarding significance of Makar Sankranti. A few selected interpretations and saying are briefly stated hereunder:

"Uttarayan is considered to be a symbol of positivity. On the other hand, Dakshinayan is considered to be a symbol of negativity. Worship, austerities, donations, charities etc. performed during these periods are of immense importance. It is believed that all these ceremonies give hundred times more results during these periods. Saur month begins from the day of Sun's Sankranti. The period from Sun's one sankranti to another is known as Saur month. A Saur year comprises of two parts - Uttarayan and Dakshinayan. Both are six month each".[9]

"Sun and Saturn are believed to be detrimental planets in the universe. They are even said to be the most dangerous and antagonistic celestial bodies and supposed to have positive and negative influences on people on Earth. On the occasion of Makar Sankranti, Sun successfully invades inside the house of Saturn who is better known to be the Lord of Capricorn sign. Sun also remains in Saturn's house for a month or so with his dear son. On account of it, Sun forgets its annoyance and pique towards Saturn and later tries to maintain a healthy relationship for Saturn and others".[10]

In an article 'Spiritual and Religious Significance of Makar Sankranti, appeared in https://astrobix.com/ the significances are highlighted as hereunder.[11]

> On the day of Makar Sankranti, sun enters into the sign of Saturn. Sun God is the father of Saturn. Father goes to meet his son in his home. Saturn and Sun, both are might planets, who's auspicious blessings can make humans achieve great success. Hence, on the holy festival of Makar Sankranti people delight sun and Saturn.

> This festival is mentioned in many of our religious text which enlighten about the festival's religious significance. The religious scripture, "Gita" which is known as the voice of Lord Krishna, illustrates that six months of Uttarayan is the day time of deity. And, the 6 months of Dakhshinayan is the night for Gods. It is believed that person who scarifies his body (dies) in Uttarayan get a position in 'Krishna Lok'. That person gets liberation, whereas, the one who dies in Dakhshinayan, has to be reborn.

> Makar Sankranti is the Festival of Truth, Virtue and Religion. Night is considered as the symbol of sin, false and wrong doings, whereas, day is regarded as the symbol of truth, virtue and religion. So, when it is day for Gods, all work of virtue are performed. The fruit of work is also good. On the day of Makar Sankrati when sun enters the Uttarayan, days become long and night becomes shorter. From this day the doors of Heaven are opened, so people celebrate the auspicious occasion.

- From the day of Makar Sankranti, the sun enters in Uttarayan resulting in long days. Married women pray to Sun God for long life of their husbands and give gifts to their elders, in return take blessing that the way days are getting longer, similarly, the life of their husbands also keep increasing.

- In the era of Mahabharata, Bhishma Pithamaha had a blessing of wish death. Although lying on the bed of arrows, he did not sacrifice his life in the Dakhsinayan, and waited for the Sun to go in Uttarayan. It is believed that on the day of Makar Sankranti, when sun entered in the Uttarayan, Bhishma Pithamaha discarded his body.

- In the case of Makar Sankranti, there is one more religious story which states that, Yashoda Mata kept fast to have Lord Krishna as her son. The story of Gangawatran is also linked with Makar Sankranti. It is said that on the day of Makar Sankranti, Ganga followed Bhagirath Muni and met the ocean. Conjunction of Ganga and ocean is the reason behind crowd of devotees taking bath in Ganagasagar on Makar Sankranti.

Significances of Kartik Sankranti

In Kartik Sankranti, the Sun enters into Tula Rashi(Libra sign) from Tula rashi (Virgo sign). During the transit, the Sun is worshiped. People wake up early in the morning of the day, offer water to the Sun and wish for their good health. Taking a dip in the holy rivers is considered to be extremely auspicious. Lighting lights in front of Tulsi and Peepal tree is regarded as of great importance.

"At the time of Tula Sankranti, grains start appearing in paddy. People offer fresh paddy to please Maa Laxmi in connection with this happiness. At some places, even twigs of wheat and Cara plants are offered to Maa Lakshmi. People pray to Maa Lakshmi to protect their crops from floods, droughts, pests etc. and provide them with an abundant crop every year. Therefore, there is a special ritual to venerate Maa Lakshmi on this day. It is believed that there is no shortage of grains if one worships Maa Lakshmi with all his/her family members and offers fresh paddy."[12]

Sun remains in Libra for almost whole month of Kartik. Therefore not only the Sankranti, but the whole month of Kati (Kartik) is considered as auspicious. This month is especially considered auspicious for flowing Chaki in the holy waters of pilgrimages like Ganges. Several festivals are celebrated in different parts of India in the month of Kartik which include Dipawali, Ahoi Ashtami, Akshaya Navami, Kartik Purnima, Bali Pratipada, Bhai Dooj, Sohrai Nag Nathaiya, Kartik Ekadashi and Gobardhan puja.

Chapter IV
RITUALS AND GAMES OF BOHAG BIHU

Performing rituals is vital part of agrarian folk festivals across the world. The word ritual means 'a set of fixed actions and sometimes words performed regularly, especially as a part of ceremony'[13]. "Rituals may be prescribed by the traditions of a community, including a religious community. Rituals are characterized, but not defined, by formalism, traditionalism, invariance, rule-governance, sacral symbolism, and performance".[14] In case of an agrarian folk festival, the rituals represent several activities and social norms related to religious faiths, social activities, cultural activities, and indigenous technical knowledge (ITK). The rituals can well be recognised as the ways and means of attaining the purposes of celebrating the festival. Moreover, some of the rituals of agrarian folk festivals are meant for growth of crops, and wellbeing of individual, family and community.

The Assamese people have been performing a wide range of rituals as part of celebrating the three Bihu festivals with great enthusiasm, faith, sincerity and carefulness. There are rituals for all different purposes of all the three festivals. In addition to spiritual and religious rituals there are several rituals are there which awake and inspire the people to mandatorily perform some crucial ancillary activities for betterment of livelihood, agriculture, crafts etc. There are rituals beneficial for interpersonal relationships, community cohesiveness and personal health. Thus, sincere execution of the rituals as part of celebrating the Bihu festivals contributes significantly not only towards spiritual, mental and physical wellbeing but also towards socio-economic prosperity and socio-cultural development. Most of the rituals of Bihu festivals are performed at family level while some of them are performed as community and as group.

Majority of the rituals of the Bihu festivals are by and large relevant and applicable in present day context too. In present day too, Assamese families across rural and urban areas perform the rituals of all the three Bihu festivals wholeheartedly, and to the possible extent. As because, Assamese race is comprised of multi-ethnic, multi-linguistic and multi-religious people, some of the rituals of Bihu festivals are performed by different communities with slight variations, but keeping main purpose and spirit the same. A couple of rituals are of course incompatible to perform in present day urban conditions.

Rituals of Xaat Bihu

The rituals of Bohag Bihu are substantially more in number, quantum and diversity as compared to that of Magh Bihu and Kati Bihu. The rituals of the festival are performed systematically for seven days. The type of main mandatory ritual to be performed in each of seven days is definite, and each day is named according to the type of mandatory ritual to be performed. The seven days together is called as Xaat Bihu. The Assamese word Xaat means seven. In a sense, Xaat Bihu can be understand as a set of prescribed rituals to be performed customarily in each of the seven days of celebrating Bohag Bihu. Adherence to the rituals of Xaat Bihu also leads people to perform certain crucial activities as part of celebrating Bohag Bihu which otherwise are generally ignored due to busy daily life and livelihood efforts. The names of the seven days are:

- ➢ Goru Bihu
- ➢ Manuh Bihu
- ➢ Kutum Bihu
- ➢ Haat Bihu
- ➢ Tantar Bihu
- ➢ Nangal Bihu
- ➢ Chera Bihu.

Of-course, among localities and communities there are couple of variations regarding names, mandated rituals and sequence of the days of Xaat Bihu. These variations are delineated at end of this heading. The rituals of each of the above mentioned seven days are stated below.

Rituals of Goru Bihu

Washing and caring of bullocks and cows is the main mandated ritual performed in the villages on the day of Goru Bihu. Of-course, there are a few other rituals and customary rituals too. The main rituals are:

- ➢ Goru–ga-dhuuwa
- ➢ Keeping Chaat, Makhioti and Dighlati
- ➢ Feasting cuisine of Chaat
- ➢ Adorning with Jetuka
- ➢ Starting Hunchari
- ➢ Feasting medicinal cuisines

Goru–ga-dhuuwa

Washing and caring of bullocks and cows is the main mandated ritual performed in the villages on the day of Goru Bihu. This set of rituals is called as Goru–ga-dhuuwa. The Assamese word Goru means bullock or cow. Throughout the day of Goru Bihu, every family with a great deal of spiritual spirit performs series of rituals with the purpose of wellbeing of bullocks and cows.

At the dawn of the day of Goru Bihu, every family with auspicious spirit starts a series of traditional preparations necessary for washing and caring of bullocks and cows. The male members of family make slices of various vegetables including Bottle-gourd, Brinjal, Cucumber, Bitter-gourd, Turmeric, Sweet potato and Borthekera

(Garcinia pedunculata). Then they stitch the slices of vegetables in a typical tool. This simple tool is made from piece bamboo strip of about 2 inches breath and 1.5 feet length by creating 2 to 5 numbers of spokes. The tool with stitched slices of vegetables is called as Chaat. It is also called as Chaatbari in some places. A family prepared 2 to 5 number of such Chaat depending on number of bullocks and cows. The stitched slices of vegetables are also called as Chaat. Once stitching of the slices of vegetables done, the pieces of Chaat kept on a Dola by placing a piece of Agoli-kolpat (tip portion of a banana leaf) on it. Dola is a big sized dish shaped bamboo-made utensil of Assamese culture. Then lumps of paste of black-gram, fresh turmeric, barbequed Borthekera and a mixture of ash and mustard oil or castor oil are kept along with the Chaat but separately. These items are generally prepared by female members of the family. Finally, one or two branches of Makhioti (Flemingia strobilfera) and Dighlati (Litsea salicifolia) plants, and new ropes to tie bullocks and cows are also kept with the chat.

On completion of the above preparations, family members take Xewa in front of the prepared materials and thereby offer those to the God(s) and pray for wellbeing of the bullocks and cows. Xewa is typical style of praying the God(s) and offering reverence to respected person or group by Hindu Assamese people. The prostration pose of Sastanga Pranam of Hinduism is followed in doing Xewa. After doing Xewa, family members used portions of the above mentioned pastes to rub on bodies of the bullocks and cows. Moreover, forehead, horns and hooves are smeared with the mixture of ash and mustard oil or castor oil. In some localities families additionally adorn bullocks and cows with garlands of sliced vegetables. In some localities families also embodied bodies of bullocks and cows by marking with the ash and oil mixture using bamboo stick or twig of the castor plant.

After completing the aforesaid ritualistic activities at home, male members of each of the families of a village or neighbourhood take the bullocks and cows to a common water source such as river, stream and Beel for washing them together with other families in festive mode, and by following definite ritualistic actions. The Dola with all the items is also taken to the water source. The branches of Makhioti and Dighlati plants are used to gently strike the bullocks and cows while driving them from home to the common source of water. It is believed that striking bullocks and cows by branches of these medicinal plants on the day of Goru Bihu protect them from various pests and diseases to a great extent for the whole year.

After washing the bullocks and cows at common source of water, family members throw Chaat (slices of vegetables) on the bullocks and cows by ushering specific rhyme for their growth and wellbeing. This very rhyme is: '*lao kha, bengena kha, bochore bochore bardhi ja; maar xoru, baaper xoru, toi ho' bor goru.*' After this action, all become busy to collect the Chaat (slices of vegetables) from the ground, and take home for preparation of a special traditional cuisine of medicinal value.

Each family takes bath on the day of Goru Bihu by applying the said pastes. In some localities, people take bath preferably in the same source of water, and while returning home pray at community place of worship. The place of worship of Hindu Assamese people is typical, and it is called as Namghar.

In the afternoon, bullocks and cows are tided in cowshed with new ropes. Generally, rope of Bamboo-leaved Galangal (*Alpinia nigra*) called in Assamese as Tora plant is used to tie bullocks and cows from the day of Goru Bihu. Then after, a medicinal smoke is arranged near cowshed for the bullocks and cows. This smoke is made by burning rice-bran and twigs of several medicinal plants including Puli-kaint (*Maclura cochinensis*), Makhioti and Dighlati. It is believed that the very smoke keeps away the pests from cowshed to a great extent for the whole year. Then each of the bullocks and cow is fed with a special kind of Laru made of rice flour and molasses or salt.

Keeping Chaat, Makhioti and Dighlati

After completion of the activities of Goru-ga-dhuuwa in community water source, every family takes back home a partially used Chaat (the tool with stitched vegetables), and also the used branches of Makhioti and Dighlati. These items are kept in safe places of cowshed and house with the belief that these auspicious items protect cattle and family from pests, diseases and other evils throughout the year.

Feasting cuisine of Chaat

In the dinner of Goru Bihu an especial traditional curry is prepared from the Chaat (the slices of vegetables collected after throwing on bullocks and cows). Usually it is prepared with eggs. This cuisine is marvellously palatable, and believed to be of great medicinal value.

Adorning with Jetuka

Jetuka (Lawsonia inermis) is a bushy plant, and paste of its leaves is used to adorn nails, fingers, palm and toe by Assamese womenfolk. It is considered as a ritual to be carried out in the evening of Goru Bihu. Young leaves of Jetuka plant are selected to make the paste which is laid on nails, fingers, palm and toe. Traditionally, the paste is kept laid for couple of hours so that the said parts of hands and feet get adorned with magenta colour. The colour generally remains for couple of months. In order to enhance intensity and durability of the colour, some people also use selected additional ingredients with Jetuka leaves to prepare the paste. Adorning the parts hands and feet with paste of Jetuka not only adds beauty but also works in protecting from diseases caused by mud and muddy water. In some families menfolk also laid paste of Jetuka on nails of thumb and big toe.

Starting Hunchari

Hunchari is initiated in courtyards of families in the evening of Goru Bihu with auspicious spirit and definite ritualistic actions. Of course, in some villages it is started in the evening of Manuh Bihu. Usually, it is started in the courtyard of the most respected personality of village.

Feasting medicinal cuisines

Feasting of traditional cuisines of medicinal value is regarded as an important ritual of Goru Bihu. Out the two kinds of traditional cuisines of medicinal value mentioned below one kind is prepared by the families at different parts of the state. It is believed that eating these cuisines on the day of Goru Bihu is beneficial for boosting immunity and keeping a person healthy for the year. In few places this ritual is followed in the day of Manuh Bihu instead of Goru Bihu.

1. **Curry of 101 herbs**: A traditional curry is prepared in the dinner of Goru Bihu from various parts of 101 selected plant species most of which are herbs. It is believed that these parts become markedly enriched with medicinal properties at the time of Bohag Bihu, and also become readily available. There are more than 101 plant species from which a family can collect the parts depending on availability in the vicinity. A list of 150 such plant species is presented with photographs in Appendix X.

2. **Curry of 7 herbs:** Instead of 101 plant species, 7 selected herbs of medicinal value are collected and prepare an especial traditional curry in the dinner of Goru Bihu. The curry is particularly popular in Lower-Assam, and it is called as Xatxaki.

Rituals of Manuh Bihu

The Assamese word Manuh means human. On this day, several mandated rituals are performed which are meant for personal wellbeing, family welfare, healthy interpersonal relationships and socio-cultural development. The main rituals listed and briefed hereunder:

- Medicinal bath and new dress
- Prayer and reverence
- Mother's especial blessings
- Exchanging love and gifts
- Eating bitter stuff
- Rejoicing breakfast together
- Purification and protection
- Taking steam of Lai-jabori
- Wearing string of turmeric leaf
- Cuisine of Red ants' eggs, larvae and pupae

Medicinal bath and new dress

Every member of the families takes bath early in the morning by applying traditional paste of medicinal value. Some families use the paste of black-gram, turmeric and barbequed Borthekera for the purpose. Some families use paste of fresh turmeric and leaves of Neem tree (Azadirachita indica). After bath, people preferably wear new dresses.

Prayer and reverence

After taking bath, every family prays the God(s) by doing Xewa for prosperity, success and peace for the year. Then after, the junior members of family do Xewa to the seniors and thereby offer reverence and obtain blessings. Customarily, while doing Xewa to convey reverence to senior in Bohag Bihu, a Guwapan or Tamulpan (one or two beetle-nut and two or three beetle vine leaves) is offered in a Xorai or Bota or Agoli-kolpat. In addition to Guwapan, a Bihuwan or a Seleng-sadar is also offered preferably. Additionally, other gift items are also offered to possible extent. Womenfolk also offer Thuria-tamul (directly consumable piece of beetle-nut and beetle vine) additionally. The senior member in return obviously offers blessings. He or she may also offer a Bihuwan and other gifts.

Later in the day, blessings are also obtained from selected relatives and respected persons of community in same manner. The Assamese word Tamul means Areca-nut and Pan means Betel-vine.

Xorai and Bota are two kinds of exquisite traditional utensils of Assamese culture. Both are generally made of bell-metal but also made from cane or wood. Xorai is mainly used to keep offerings in prayer to God(s) or in conveying reverence to a person or group. Bota is a daily used utensil in which mainly Tamul-pan is kept and offered. At present, Xorai is also used as an emblematic decorative piece of Assamese culture, and to felicitate honourable personality.

Seleng-sadar is a specially woven prototypical costume of Assamese culture used by both menfolk and womenfolk in special occasions including of Bohag Bihu. It is also considered as an honorary piece of costume, and used as a special gift item to offer to respected persons in various occasions.

Mother's especial blessings

It is one of the most distinctive and high value rituals of Bohag Bihu. In this ritual, on the day of Manuh Bihu the sons and daughters receive blessings from their mother especially. Sons and daughters do Xewa to mother in order to offer reverence at the occasion of the festival. Generally a Guwapan with a Seleng-sadar or a Bihuwan are offered in a Xorai or Bota or Agoli-kolpat while doing Xewa to mother. Other kinds of gifts are also offered to the possible extent. In return, mother offers them not only blessings, and but also gives breeze of Bichani which is a traditional tool made of bamboo or cane used as manually operated fan. It is believed that the breeze of Bichani from mother on the day of Manuh Bihu immensely benefits her sons and daughters in keeping good health and peace of mind throughout the year. In addition to blessings and breeze of Bichani, mother also offers Bihuwan to sons and daughters. Quite obviously, this very ritual is enriched with superb wisdom, and hence, especial attention is to be put to perform this ritual wholeheartedly. As because, this superlative ritual bears brilliant wisdom, so, can also be regarded as a matter of pride for Assamese people.

Exchanging love and gifts

Offering of love and gifts to lover, spouse, brother, sister, aunt, and close friends is also considered as a mandated ritual to be performed on the day of Manuh Bihu. Traditionally female offers Bihuwan to male loved one, while male offers attractive gifts. As said earlier, Kopouphul is considered as an especial gift from boyfriend to lover or husband to wife.

Eating bitter stuff

Eating selected bitter foodstuff at empty stomach is regarded as a ritual to be followed in the day of Manuh Bihu. It is believed that this ritual benefits greatly in protecting from stomach and skin diseases. There are a few traditional options of the bitter foodstuff:

> Juice of Neem tree leaves, tender pine apple leaves and raw turmeric.

> Paste of lentil and tender leaves of mango tree.

> ➤ Juice of leaves and twigs of Vasaka (Justicia adhatoda) plant.

Rejoicing breakfast together

After completion of the above stated rituals in the morning, family members take breakfast together with varieties of traditional sweets and refreshments mentioned earlier.

Purification and protection

There are a few rituals performed in Manuh Bihu by some of families in different parts of Assam with the purpose of purification and protection of house, family and cattle-shed.

> ➤ Some families write selected auspicious verses on leaves of Iron tree and keep them in selected places of house. It is based on the belief that so written verses foster all round wellbeing of family, and also protect family from all different evils.

> ➤ Some families make a bunch of twigs of certain medicinal plants, and used that bunch to sprinkle water all around the house. The bunch is then kept inserted into the rafters of the roofs. Some other families sprinkle with juice of basil leaves on the cattle-shed and around the house.

> ➤ Some families hang a small bundle containing pieces of onion, unripe mango, and Gulanch(*Plumeria acuminta*) flower at certain places of the house. Some families make bunches of twigs or shoots of various bitter plants and are placed at different places of house, cattle-shed and homestead. It is believed that the bitter plant-materials keep snakes away.

Taking steam of Lai-jabori

In this ritual each member of a family inhale steam of a kind of vegetable called Lai-jabori (Drymaria cordalata). It is believed that inhaling steam of this particular vegetable on the day of Manuh Bihu protects from diseases of nose and head throughout the year.

Wearing string of turmeric leaf

This ritual is called as Choita-bao, and followed in some places. A string is made from midrib of died turmeric leaf, and children and young people wear the same around waist. It is believed that the string protects from evil spirits and diseases.

Cuisine of Red ants' eggs, larvae and pupae

On the day of Manuh Bihu, some of the families in certain parts of the state prepare and rejoice a superbly palatable traditional cuisine from eggs, larvae and pupae of Weaver ant (red), *Oecophylla smaragdina*, commonly called as Red ant. The Assamese name of this species of ant is Amroli-porua. The eggs, larvae and pupae are collected from their nests in trees. Nests of Amroli-porua at mango and jackfruit trees are preferred for the purpose. It is believed that eggs, larvae and pupae of Amroli-porua are highly nutritious and of high medicinal value. The traditional indigenous knowledge (ITK) associated is that feasting of this very cuisine particularly on the day of Manuh Bihu protects from diseases like malaria, jaundice, and nose related diseases. The cuisine is of slight citrusy taste, lemony flavour and awe-inspiringly palatable.

The cuisines of eggs, larvae and pupae of Asian weaver ants are popular delicacies in Lao PDR, Thailand, South America and in parts of Kerela.[15,16,17,18] In several parts of Thailand and Lao PDR the eggs, larvae and pupae of Asian weaver ants are widely used as an important, nutritious and medicinal food ingredient. The people of the regions use several traditional methods of collecting the brood of Asian weaver ants from their nests in the nature. "Certain kinds, especially the larvae and pupae of the weaver ant, are in high demand in Asia. They're considered a delicacy in parts of South America, where some of the top chefs often use them in high-end dishes. A good source of protein, they're said to have a lemony, citrusy flavor".[19]

Couple of scientific studies have proved nutritious values of eggs, larvae and pupae of Asian weaver ant (red), Oecophylla smaragdina. In a study carried out in Thailand by a group of researchers report that eggs, larvae and pupae of Asian weaver ants have high nutritional values and comprise 53% protein and 13% lipid. Peptides derived from food proteins have been shown to possess biological activities.[20] "Another study carried out on this foodstuff of tribal groups residing in the forests of Wayanadu and Kasaragod districts of Kerala, India reported detailed findings: 'Adult worker ants possess high formic acid (FA) content in their abdominal poison gland reservoir. Oecophylla brood has no traces of FA, but possesses all the essential amino acids, especially tryptophan, leucine, threonine, methionine and lysine in high concentration. Brood also has high carbohydrate content and very low lipid content. Carbohydrate, protein and lipid exist in a ratio 5: 2.5: 1 on wet weight basis. Brood is a rich source of retinol, tocopherol, ascorbic acid, thiamine, niacin and riboflavin, which are present at several times higher concentration than that of the egg of domestic fowl. Among various minerals tested, Na, P, Ca and Mg were present in very high concentration".[21]

Thus, the ritual of enjoying delicacy of the cuisine prepared from eggs, larvae and pupae can well be regarded as scientifically nutritious and medicinal, and there might be scientific validity of the traditional belief that it protects from malaria, jaundice and nose related diseases. Moreover, as the cuisine is marvellously palatable there is scope to commercially utilize this cuisine as a traditional Assamese delicacy. It is encouraging that couple of entrepreneurs are putting effort in this direction. However, the need of sustainable cultivation for sufficiency of the raw material along with techniques of harvesting might be crucial requirement for its wide range commercial use.

Ritual of Kutum Bihu

On this day of Kutum Bihu people do visit to close relatives. Particularly, newly married daughter with her spouse as well as kids visits her parents' house. Special traditional dishes are prepared for them. Exchange of gifts along with love and respect takes place among members of both the families. Kutum Bihu is also called as Senehi Bihu in some localities.

Ritual of Tantar Bihu

Cleaning of the parts of weaving set is the mandated ritual of this day. After cleaning the parts, the female member of family take Xewa in front of the parts of weaving set, and worship. Weaving is a glorious tradition of Assamese culture. Assamese women are superbly skilful and talented in weaving various costumes, and to create varieties of beautiful traditional floral pattern. Traditionally, weaving is considered as envisaged skill of an Assamese woman. The varieties of traditional floral patterns so far created by Assamese women across centuries are regarded as a glorious heritage.

Ritual of Haat Bihu

On this day, people visit friends and relatives as part of celebrating the festival. Such visits may or may not be as per invitations. Warm hospitality along with Pitha, Laru and Jalpan are offered whoever visits a family. In some places this day is also called as Mela Bihu.

Ritual of Nangal Bihu

The Assamese word Nangal means plough, the main implement for land preparation in crop cultivation. On the day of Nangal Bihu, all the agricultural implements are cleaned and kept ready to use. After cleaning the implements, the family members take Xewa in front of the implements, and pray God(s).

Ritual of Chera Bihu

The Assamese word Chera means last one. It is the last day of celebrating Bohag Bihu. Thus, it can be considered as closing ceremonial day. Particularly, Hunchari is closed for the year ceremonially on this day by following definite ritualistic actions. The Hunchari-dal of each village performs Hunchari in an open field for hours, and thus closes Hunchari programme for the year. The rituals of Chera Bihu help people to switch their attention from fun and joy to the livelihood activities, and to rejuvenate enthusiasm to involve themselves in activities of on-coming cultivation of *Sali*-paddy.

Variations relating to Xaat Bihu

As mentioned earlier there are couple of variations among localities and communities regarding names, mandated rituals and sequence of the days of Xaat Bihu. Some of the families observe the 3ʳᵈ day of as Gonshai-Bihu instead of Kutum Bihu. In some localities, people called the day of Tantar Bihu as Maiki Bihu and perform additional ritualistic activities. Some of the families club the rituals of Tantar Bihu and Nangal Bihu together, and observe the day as Nangal Bihu. In some places people observe a day for animals and birds and called as Poxu-pakhi Bihu. However, the names and rituals of first two days and last day are same everywhere. The rituals of Gonshai Bihu, Maiki Bihu and Poxu-pakhi Bihu are briefly presented below.

Ritual of Gonshai Bihu

As stated earlier, some families observe 3ʳᵈ day of Bohag Bihu as Gonshai Bihu. The mandatory ritual of this day is to visit Gonshai (religious guru) for offering reverence and gifts, and obtaining blessings. Some of the families visit nearby religious places instead of visiting Gonshai.

Ritual of Maiki Bihu

In some of places, one the seven days is celebrated as Maiki Bihu. On the day, womenfolk enjoy the day by singing Bihunam and performing Bihunach.

Ritual of Poxu-pakhi Bihu

Families of some localities observe the 5th day of Bohag Bihu as Poshu-pakhi Bihu by the, and they don't observe Tantar Bihu as a separate day. However, the mandated ritual of Tantar Bihu is performed on the day of Nangal Bihu. The domesticated and wild animals and birds are fed on this day. The Assamese word Poxu means animals and Pakhi means birds. Thus, Poxu-pakhi Bihu is the day for caring animals and birds.

Rejoicing Poita-Bhat

Poita-Bhat is an archetypical meal of Assamese culture. It is prepared by dipping steamed rice overnight. It is rejoiced by adding salt, mustard oil, chilli and especially with barbequed fish. Ritualistically people start rejoicing Poita-Bhat on any of the seven days of Bohag Bihu, and takes it periodically till end of summer season. It is beneficial to bear hot in summer days.

Traditional games of Bohag Bihu

As part of celebrating Bohag Bihu, two games are organised in the villages in which menfolk take part. They are Koni-yunj (Egg-fighting) and Cowry-khel. Both are played by following archetypal traditional rules.

Koni-yunj

This prototypical game called as Koni-junj is organised at village level at the occasion of Bohag Bihu. The Assamese words Koni means egg(s), and Junj means fight. The game takes place in a common place and menfolk participated with great enthusiasm. The basic norm is that between two players who can break another's egg wins, and gets the broken egg. However, quite a few ways, norms and tricks are associated with the game, and these make it quite interesting. In some villages, Koni-junj is organised on the day of Goru Bihu while in some others on Manuh Bihu, and in some villages in both the days. This game is so interesting and tempting that till the end of 20ᵗʰ century, in many villages it was informally held a few days ahead of commencing the festival.

Cowry-khel

It is played by using cowrie shells, and so called as Cowrie-khel. The Assamese word Khel means game. The game is basically similar to that of Pachisi disc game of Indian culture but distinctively different in regard to purpose and conditions. The board of the game is same with Pachisi disc game which is symmetrical cross shaped. As like Pachisi disc game, Cowry-khel is also played with 6 small cowry shells as dice, and by following same rules.

As part of celebrating Bohag Bihu, the Cowry-khel is held between two groups of men, and played for hours in night. There is no limit of total number of players. Generally, it is organised on fifth day of the festival, and after one or two days of playing the game, all the players enjoy a feast. The most distinctive feature is that the winning group has to contribute substantially more than losing group for the feast. The board of Cowry-khel is generally prepared temporarily on floor of a house. In case of some villages, a family invites menfolk of the village to play Cowry-khel in its residence with the belief that it is auspicious and brings prosperity. In such a case, the family arrange for everything including the feast.

Chapter V

RITUALS AND GAMES OF MAGH BIHU AND KATI BIHU

This chapter presents the rituals of Magh Bihu, the rituals of Kati Bihu and the traditional games of Magh Bihu under 3 broad heads.

Rituals of Magh Bihu

The rituals of Magh Bihu are related to thanksgiving God(s), gaining mental and physical strengths, community feast, fun and joy in group, enjoying bone fire, and feasting traditional cuisines, Pitha, Laru and Jalpan. The main rituals are:

- Bhelaghar
- Community feast
- Community fishing
- Mezi
- Binding fruit plants
- Prayer and reverence
- Feasting traditional delicacies

The rituals are briefly stated hereunder, and photographs of selected rituals and games of Magh Bihu and Kati Bihu are presented in Appendix II.

Bhelaghar and community feast

Bhelaghar is a typical makeshift cottage made of rice straw and bamboo. Before commencing Magh Bihu a group of young menfolk of each of the villages or neighbourhoods construct a Bhelaghar. The group of young menfolk stay in Bhelaghar in the night of Uruka of Magh Bihu, and enjoy whole night by singing, dancing, making fun, enjoying warmth of bone fire, and rejoicing traditional foodstuff.

A community feast is arranged in the evening of Uruka in the vicinity of Bhelaghar. Generally all members of the families of the village or neighbourhood enjoy the feast together. Thanksgiving to God for the harvest is an essential part of this feast. It is arranged plenteously with various traditional cuisines particularly of duck meat and big fishes.

Community fishing

On the day of Uruka or day before Uruka of Magh Bihu, in some places people of several villages harvest fish together in common water source like river and Beel. Harvested fishes are mainly used for the community feasts.

Mezi–the prototypical bone fire

Mezi is an archetypically arranged big sized bonfire. It is generally organised by the side of Bhelaghar. It is arranged by staking riven pieces of wood logs in a definite shape that gradually tapered upward. Traditionally 4 trees of banana are put at four corners of the stake, and provision is made at the base so as to put fire from four sides by using four bunches dried bamboo sticks. Such a bunch of dried bamboo sticks is called as Jumuthi. There is no very definite size of Mezi. Even so, height of a Mezi of standard size is not less than 7 feet. The activities of arranging Mezi usually begins well ahead of Uruka as because the riven pieces of wood logs have to be dried enough for easy burning even in heavily foggy condition of early morning of Magh Bihu. Instead of banana trees at four corners of the stake of riven wood, bamboo trees or Areca-nut trees are also used in some localities.

Mezi is considered as auspicious and hence, its arrangement is started with a prayer to God(s) by doing Xewa. It is burnt at the dawn of the day of Magh Bihu, and the people enjoy warmed with auspicious spirit. It is believed that the warmth of Mezi renounces lethargy caused by chilling winter, and provides strength to be zestful in coming days. One has to take bath mandatorily to put fire on Mezi, or to take its warmth. The God or a demigod namely Agni is worshiped while putting fire on Mezi. Some of the communities usher specific spiritual verses as special prayer at this auspicious occasion. Some people put rice, Pitha, Laru, Tamul-pan, sesames on fire of Mezi as offering to the God or Agni deity. People take ash and burnt pieces at the end for throwing on fruit plants with the belief that the practice is beneficial for getting more and good quality fruits.

In some places fire crackers are made by putting water in bamboo internodes, and put in the midst of the riven pieces of wood logs of Mezi. Such a cracker bursts with big sound when gets burnt, and thus fun is created.

There is another type of Mezi too which is arranged in some of the villages. It is made of rice straw. The size of such a Mezi is generally much bigger than the Mezi of wood logs. Its flame last for much lesser time as compared to that of riven pieces of wood logs. Warmth of a Mezi of wood log can be enjoyed even after 24 hours. In some villages both the types of Mezi are arranged. In few villages another type of Mezi is also arranged which is made of dried banana leaves. It is of course arranged as additional one.

Binding fruit plants

In the early morning of Magh Bihu every family loosely bind fruit plants of homestead with rope made from paddy straw or fibre of banana stem. Then family members throw small lumps of soil on the fruit plants and ushers a specific phrase to express wish that plants bear fruits profusely.

Prayer and reverence

After enjoying warmth of Mezi, people go back home, and at first pray God(s) as a family together. Then after junior members do Xewa to offer convey reverence to seniors in traditional manner. In the afternoon Community prayer and worship programme is held in Namghar of each of the villages.

Feasting traditional delicacies

After completion of prayer and offering reverence to seniors, the family members take breakfast together with Pitha, Laru and Jalpan. Moreover, delicacy of several typical species of potato is especially enjoyed in the breakfast of Magh Bihu, and it is regarded as a mandated ritual. The local names of some of these potato species are Mitha-alu (Ipomoea batatas), Kath-alu (Dioscorea alata), Mua-alu, Simalu-alu, Ada-alu. Assamese word alu means potato. These typical species of potato become mainly available during the season of Magh Bihu. There are several kinds of traditional recipes to prepare those and they are enjoyed not only on the days of the festival but for couple of months. A traditional belief associated with this ritual is that if someone does not take such a typical species of potato in Magh Bihu, he or she becomes like pig for the year. Pig here implies voracious eater. The said species of potato are also barbequed in fire of Mezi and bone-fire of Bhelaghar, and enjoyed.

Inviting of friends and relatives and offering warm hospitality with Pitha, Laru, Jalpan and especial traditional cuisines is also regarded as customary rituals of Magh Bihu.

Rituals of Kati Bihu

There are two kinds of rituals of Kati Bihu for two significant purposes of the festival. In the afternoon of Kati Bihu, each agrarian family puts oil-based lamps called as Chaki at different places of the plots of *Sali*-paddy crop, and worships God(s) to protect the crop from pests and other evils. The lamps attract the pests, and many of them get killed by the flames of the lamps, and thus they evidently work as a control measure of pests in the crop field. Moreover, some people believe that Lakshmi, the Goddess of prosperity is pleased with the light of lamps, thereby bestows blessings. In some places lamps are put in vegetable garden too. Some of the families in some places sing specific hymns while performing this ritual.

> As said earlier, another purpose of celebrating Kati Bihu is obtaining blessings of God(s) particularly of Goddess Lakshmi for prosperity and safety of family. With this purpose, every family puts Chaki in front of courtyard and in front of a basil plant, and worship God(s) or Goddess Lakshmi. Specific hymns are sung while worshiping. In this ritual, some families sung definite hymns as part of worshiping the Goddess Lakshmi. Females take leading roles in performing both the rituals of Kati Bihu.

> In some places some families also traditionally follow additional or alternative methods as ritual of Kati Bihu with the purpose of protecting crops from pests and other evils. Four such methods are as hereunder:

> In some localities, some farmers recite certain mantras at own plots of *Sali*-paddy crop with the help of a kind of convalescent professional. The professional is called as Bej in Assamese. The Bej sings definite mantras and the farmer repeat the same. This ritual is performed with the belief that the specific mantras bind the mouths of animals, birds, rodents, insects etc. and thus, crop gets protected.

> In some places some farmer buried a pair of mouse in a spot of the crop field.

> In a few places, farmers hang sky-lamps called as Akash-bonti in Paddy field. Lights (Chaki) are put at tip of tall bamboo poles. It is generally arranged as group or community level.

> ➤ In a few localities farmers arrange a typical flame by using jute stick. It is made by tying some cotton or fibre of jute at the tip of long jute stick, and then soaked in oil, and then lit fire to produce flame. It is called as Bhoga-dewa. The flamed sticks are placed at several spots of the crop field so that pests are attracted and died.

Traditional games of Magh Bihu

The main typical game organised during Magh Bihu is Moh-yunj means Buffalo-fight. Other traditional games organised as part of celebrating Magh Bihu are – Bulbuli–junj(Nightingale-fight), Cock-fight, Dhop-khel, Tekeli-phutuwa, Olong-danlong, Tang-guti, Thengal-dour, Dhora-hao, Boha-hao. A brief description of Moh-yunj and Bulbuli-yunj is placed hereunder:

Moh-yunj and Bulbuli-yunj

On occasion of Magh Bihu people arranged fights of pairs of domesticated buffaloes in harvested paddy fields and enjoy the fights. It is called as Moh-junj. Moh means buffalo(s). Domesticated water buffaloes are important resource in agrarian Assamese society as both draught and milch animal. The water buffalo gain maximum strength at the time of Magh Bihu as because fodders in nature become easily and abundantly available in the season. With enough physical strength buffaloes particularly male ones become prone to fight each other.

Buffalo-fights were held in considerable number of villages till 2014. However, due to the ordinance passed in the Supreme Court of India in 2014 which banned all kinds of staged fights between animals, the buffalo-fights in the state reduced drastically.

Fights between pairs of Bulbuli (Nightingale) birds (Pycnonotus cafer), were also organised as a tradition in a few villages at the occasion of Magh Bihu. It was organised and conducted by skilled persons with specific preparations. However, this game and also Cock-fight have abolished almost completely due to the above mentioned ordinance of the Supreme Court of India.

Chapter VI

BIHUBADYA

The musical instruments accompanied with Bihunam and Bihunach are called as Bihubadya. They are of seven types:

1. Bihu-dhol

2. Mohor-xingar-penpa

3. Toka

4. Gogona

5. Xutuli

6. Pati-tal

7. Baanhi.

Claps are also substantially accompanied with Bihunam and Bihunach in addition to the Bihubadhya. Out of the seven Bihubadya the first 5 are prototypical of Assamese culture. They are made from locally available materials by skilled artisans. This chapter presents brief description of each Bihubadya.

Bihu-dhol

It is a membranophone type of instrument consists of total 12 components. The drum is made of wood, and the membranes fitted at two mouths of the drum are made of cow's skin. The instrument is played by hitting the membrane of the left mouth of the drum by palm, and by hitting the membrane of other mouth with a typical stick made of bamboo. Varieties of mnemonic syllables called as *bols* are produced. Moreover, a kind of *bol* is also produced by hitting body of the drum with the stick. The word *bol* is a term used in Indian classical music: "Words or syllables implied in Taala. The term also means syllables of instruments – it may be percussion, string or wind instruments or the syllables in a song".[22] A Taala literally means a clap, tapping one›s hand on one›s arm, a musical measure».[23] "It is the term used in Indian classical music to refer to musical meter".[24]

Bols of Bihu-dhol

Many *bols* including closed *bols*, open *bols* and combined *bols* are produced by playing Bihu-dhol. The *bols* of Bihu-dhol are similar to that of Indian membranophone type of musical instruments such as Khol, Mridang and Tabla but not the same. Moreover, substantially more numbers of *bols* can be produced by playing Bihu-dhol as compared to that of Khol, Mridang and Tabla. The *bols* of Bihu-dhol produced while playing with Bihunach and Bihunam include: *ta, da, ti, ni, gi, ghi, dhin, ghin, ghen, gu, tak, dak, khit, khita, khiti, tidhi, tikhi, idi, ikhi, taki, takhi, daki, khita, nita, niti, ghigi, nakhi, naghi, ghen, righen, gheni, ghenit, khitir, khikhir, dakhir, khitin, ghiniti, tighen, righen, nighen, khir, duru, gudu, uru, ururu, daun, taun, jaun, taghen, ghinau, khitau, khikhau, didau, ghenau, udau, dhindau, khitau, ghendau, ghnuuu etc.*

Cheu of Bihu-dhol

When a definite set of *bols* is played in a definite construction and rhythm(s) in Bihu-dhol, the Bandish so produced is called as Dholar-cheu. Bandish is a term used in Hindustani music: "A composition in Raga music. This term is broadly used for any type of composition in Hindustani Art music- even rhythmic compositions are referred as bandish".[25] The term *bajna* is used as a synonym of Bandish.

It is quite obvious that in order to perform Bihunach precisely on any Dholar-cheu, one need to recall that thoroughly. There are mainly seven types of Dholar-cheu and each has specific name. They are as follows:

- Khnora-cheu

- Nachoni-cheu

- Digholia-cheu

- Dutia-cheu

- Budra-cheu

- Hurali-cheu

- Kanhi-ghuruwa-cheu.

Out of the 7 types of Dholar-cheu, the Budra-cheu and Hurali-cheu are most extensive, distinctive and definitely structured. Both are played in Hunchari. The Bihunach performed in these two Dholar-cheu is definitely structured with definite movements and poses. Only the Bihuwa perform Bihunach in these two Dholar-cheu; Bihuwati do not dance. The word Bihuwa means a boy or man who participates in Hunchari and/or Bihu -competitions. Bihuwa also means a boy or man who performs Bihunach, sings Bihunam, and/or plays Bihubadya. Similarly, Bihuwati means a girl or woman who participates in Rati Bihu, Jeng Bihu, and/or Bihu-competitions. Bihuwati also means a girl or woman who performs Bihunach, sings Bihunam, and/or plays Bihubadya. The words Bihuwa and Bihuwati are used in the book as both singular and plural.

Budra-cheu consists of total 13 definitely structured *bajna*. Out of them one is called *Mul-bajna* and each of the rest 12 is called as Xnachar. The *Mul-bajna* is played at first, and also played after each Xnachar. The dance performed in each of these *bajna* is definite and precisely structured. Thus, Budra-cheu is comprised of 13 different definite *bajna* in which 13 definitely structured Bihunach are performed by Bihuwa in Hunchari. Moreover, typical Bihunam are also sung as integral part of Budra-cheu in a rhythm which is different from the rhythm of singing general Bihunam. The Bihunach performed with the Bihunam of Budra-cheu is also typical.

Hurali-cheu consists of total 6 precisely structured definite *bajna* produced by playing the Bihu-dhol. The Bihunach in each of these six *bajna* is different, and precisely structured. Typical Bihunam are sung in specific rhythm at end of each *bajna*, and the Bihunach performed in the Bihunam is also of typical style.

Each of other types of Dholar-cheu namely, Khnora cheu, Nachoni-cheu, Digholia cheu, Dutiya-cheu and Kanhi–ghuruwa-cheu are comprised of one *bajna*. In Dutia-cheu two Bihuwa perform Bihunach. As because, Khnora cheu, Nachoni-cheu and Digholia cheu are basically played in Hunchari, originally Bihuwa perform Bihunach in those in general style. In present era, Bihuwati also perform Bihunach in these three types of Dholar-cheu. On the other hand, difference of opinions exists among researchers and practitioners in case of Kanhi–ghuruwa-cheu. According to one school of thought only Bihuwa should dance in Kanhi–ghuruwa-cheu while, according to another school of thought both Bihuwa and Bihuwati can dance.

Oja-Dhol-badan of Bihu-dhol

Words can also be produced by playing Bihu-dhol. That is why, it is said that Bihu-dhol can speak, and Bihu-dhol can bring storm and rain. It is possible basically because varieties of *bols* can be produced by playing Bihu-dhol. This very advantage signifies how well developed this prototypical membranophone type traditional musical instrument of rich Assamese culture.

There is a specific format of playing Bihu-dhol in which words and phrases are produced. This format is called as Oja-Dhol-badan of Bihu-dhol. This format is not played as accompanied music of Bihunach and Bihunam but in other occasions particularly in marriage ceremony. Quite obviously, this very format reflects more strongly, clearly and convincingly how definitely prototypical is the Bihu-dhol, and how wide-ranging is its playing. It also reveals superlative talent of Assamese folk artists in playing Bihu-dhol. Oja-Dhol-badan is therefore recognised as one of the glorious prototypical cultural heritages of Assamese culture - a pride of the race.

In Oja-Dhol-badan, several definite *bajna* along with archetypal songs are presented by a team of 2 to 4 artists. The main artist is called as Oja, who plays 3 to 5 numbers of Bihu-dhol synchronously and also leads the songs. The other artists play Pati-tal, and support Oja in singing songs. There are mainly 3 types of presentations in Oja-Dhol-badan. They ate Haat, Buloni and Ghaat. Among them Haat is more extensive and definite. There are total 24 numbers of traditional Haat. In a Buloni, the team of artists narrates story or event in lyrical form called as Malita(Ballad).

Oja-Dhol-badan is an age-old tradition, and one has to learn it through meticulous training. Guru-sisya Parampara, the ancient Indian tradition system of learning is still prevailing in case of learning Oja-Dhol-badan, and there are several established norms to follow to learn the skills and present the same. Earlier only males learnt and performed Oja-Dhol-badan. However, in recent years females are also coming forward to learn and perform.

Mohor-xingar-penpa

It is an aerophone type of musical instrument, and consists of four components. One of the components is of horn of buffalo. In Assamese language buffalo is called as Moh and horn as *xing* while the word Penpa means trumpet kind of musical instrument. Thus, the name of the instrument is Mohor-xingar-penpa, in short Penpa. A few definite sets of bols with definite rhythm are produced by playing this instrument, and such a set is called Penpar-cheu. Moreover, tunes of Bihunam are also produced by playing this instrument. The music produced by playing this prototypical Bihubadhya is amazingly appealing and distinctive. Mohor-xingar-penpa is of two types: One type is of one horn, so called as Gutia-penpa. Another type is of two horns, and called as Juria-penpa.

Toka

Toka is a distinctive prototypical musical instrument of Assamese culture, and can be categorised as of percussion type. It is made from one or more internodes of bamboo by creating a pair of clappers, and played by clapping the clappers. Toka is accompanied mainly with singing Bihunam. It is of two types. One is smaller and played by taking in hands, and called Haat-toka; the Assamese word Haat means hand. Another type is bigger and played by keeping one end at floor. It is called Mati-toka. The word Mati means land or soil. Haat-toka is used by both Bihuwati and Bihuwa and played in Rati Bihu, Jeng Bihu and Hunchari. On the other hand, Mati-toka is played by Bihuwati, and was used in Rati Bihu and Jeng Bihu.

Gogona

It is another prototypical musical instrument of Assamese culture. This lamellophone type of instrument is made from a spike of bamboo of about 10 inch in length and 1 inch width. A tongue or reed is cut out at the middle. There are two types of Gogona, one is having a rope attached to one end, and another is without rope. The sound is produced by vibrating the reed by playing the instrument skilfully using both mouth and finger synchronically. It is mainly played by both Bihuwati and Bihuwa.

Xutuli

Xutuli is another prototypical musical instrument of Assamese culture made of clay soil. This simple flute type aerophone kind of musical instrument has three holes, one at middle others at two sides. Air is blown by mouth through the middle hole, and tune is maintained by playing fingers on other two holes. It is played by both Bihuwati and Bihuwa, and considered as important Bihubadhya of Rati Bihu and Jeng Bihu.

Pati-tal

It is a percussion musical instrument consists of two cymbals made of bell metal. Diameter of each cymbal is of about 6 inches having protuberance at middle portion. It is accompanied with all other Bihubadhya.

Baanhi

It is a fipple flute or end blown flute, and made from a piece of single hollow shaft of bamboo of about half inch diameter and one foot long. It is called Bansuri in Hindustani music. The tune is maintained by playing fingers on six numbers of finger-holes.

Chapter VII

GLORIOUS RATI BIHU AND JENG BIHU

Both the Rati Bihu and Jeng Bihu were held in the midst of nature in many of the villages of the Brahmaputra valley of Assam since pre-historic period to mid of 20th century. Due to changed socio-cultural, educational, economic, political and occupational circumstances most villages started refraining from organising these programmes since independence of India. At present they are not held in midst of nature, but are showcased in mock form in the cultural functions organised as part of celebration of Bohag Bihu. Both the programmes have also been showcasing in other cultural events within and outside the state, and also in abroad, and gaining great applaud. There is dearth of historical facts to ascertain exactly when these programmes were first held. However majority of the researchers opined that programme of Bihunach was held in many villages of the Brahmaputra valley since pre-historic period. Both these programmes are glorious from several perspectives.

This chapter presents brief description of each of these amazing programmes and also highlights why Rati Bihu and Jeng Bihu are regarded as glorious heritages of Assamese culture.

Rati Bihu

Rati Bihu was held under a tree or in midst of dense bamboo plantation in nights of the month of Cho't of Assamese calendar. As held in night, so, the name is Rati Bihu. The Assamese word Rati means night. A group of grown-up girls and grown-up boys were participated in Rati Bihu. The very spot at which the group girls performed Bihunach along with singing Bihunam and playing selected Bihubadhya was called as Bihukhola. The boys participated by positioning themselves as a separate group and by maintaining decent distance from Bihukhola. The group of boys sang Bihunam and played Mohor-xingar-penpa. The girls played Mati-toka, Haat-toka, Gagana and Xutuli. In a few villages, Bihu-dhol and Pati-tal were also played by the group of boys. However, it was found in an investigative study carried out by author of this book in early part of the decade of eighties of 20th century that in Rati Bihu of majority of the villages Bihu-dhol and Pati-tal were not used.

Even though Rati Bihu was not a religious event, it was started with auspicious spirit by worshiping God(s) in ritualistic manner. A Bihuwan was tied at the trunk of the big tree or bamboo plant under which Bihukhola is arranged. Then the group of girls worshiped God by ushering spiritual hymns, and thus started the event. It was also called as Ch'tor-Bihu as held for several days in the month of Cho't. Generally started in early days of the month of Cho't and continued till end of the month. In each of the days, the programme was held for several hours, and in some days continued up-to dawn. There was no limit regarding size of the groups of the girls and boys in Rati Bihu.

The Bihunam of Rati Bihu were mostly romantic, and some of those were sensual too. Of course, some of the Bihunam were on other subject-matters such as nature, culture, life style, cultivation, birds, rain, stream, river etc. One of the distinctive aspects regarding Bihunam of Rati Bihu is that boys and girls exchanged their romantic feelings and answered romantic questions by means of Bihunam. When Bihunam are sung in this way called as Joranam. Usually several verses of Bihunam were sung by pairs of a girl and boy with support of companions, and thereby expressed romantic feelings and responded to each other's questions. Often such verses of Bihunam were composed instantly. It is obvious that Joranam of Rati Bihu facilitated boys and girls to confirm or deny proposals of love. Moreover, they facilitated lovers to confirm decision to start married life. Some pairs of lovers even started married life instantly after participating in Rati Bihu.

Jeng Bihu

Jeng Bihu was held at daytime under a tree or in midst of bamboo plants, or in a bushy place. A group of grown up girls performed Bihunach along with singing Bihunam and playing Bihubadhya. The types of Bihubadhya played by the girls were Haat-toka, Mati-toka, Gogona and Xutuli. The very spot at which dancing and singing took place was called as Bihukhola – as in the case with Rati Bihu.

It was also called as Toka Bihu, Gabhoru Bihu, and Jeng Bihu. Toka was the main Bihubadhya of Jeng Bihu, so called as Toka Bihu. The word Gabhoru means a grown up girl. So, the programme was also called Gabhoru Bihu. The Assamese world Jeng means dear girl or woman, so the name is Jeng Bihu. There was no participation or involvement of menfolk in Jeng Bihu.

The way of starting the programme was the same as that of Rati Bihu. It was also started with auspicious spirit by worshiping God(s) in ritualistic manner, and by tying a Bihuwan at the trunk of the big tree or bamboo plant under which Bihukhola is arranged. In some localities Jeng Bihu was held in the month of Ch'ot for few days, and in some other localities during the seven days of celebrating Bohag Bihu starting from third day to seventh day. In some villages younger girls also organised the same programme separately. There was no limit regarding size of the group of the girls in Jeng Bihu.

The Bihunam sang in Jeng Bihu were mostly romantic but not sensual. Bihunam on subject-matters including natural beauty, culture, life style, livelihood, day to day activities, birds, streams, rivers and the like were also sung substantially.

Both Rati Bihu and Jeng Bihu were also called as Gostolor Bihu, Bonor Bihu and Maiki Bihu. The Assamese word Gostolor means below tree, so, name is Gostolor Bihu. The word bon means nature – as both the programmes were held in nature, so, Bonor Bihu. The word Maiki means women. As girls were the main participants in the programmes, so, called as Maiki Bihu.

Why are Rati Bihu and Jeng Bihu glorious?

Rati Bihu and Jeng Bihu can very well be regarded as a glorious tradition of Assamese culture from the following perspectives:

> ➤ Rati Bihu and Jeng Bihu reveal the independence and high status of women in agrarian Assamese culture. It also reflects gender equality and dignity of women in the society. The same status is prevailing even today – women are mostly regarded equally in Assamese society. The dowry system prevailing in some other Indian societies does not exist in Assamese culture.

> ➤ Rati Bihu and Jeng Bihu also depict high etiquette and moral character of Assamese people. As ascertained through investigative studies, nothing happened in Rati Bihu and Jeng Bihu which can be considered as detrimental to girls' prestige and status. Of course, as said above, Rati Bihu facilitated lovers to start married life, and some pairs started married life instantly after participating in Rati Bihu with consent of both.

> ➤ Rati Bihu and Jeng Bihu also reflect the strength of social norms in Assamese agrarian society. Although Rati Bihu was held in forest in night, the group of boys always kept decent distance from girls group by abiding the rule strictly. Both the programmes were initiated with auspicious spirit, and regarded as modest. The participating groups of boys and girls were keen and sensible to keep prestige of village as well as society.

> ➤ These programmes also reveal high standard of social fabrics prevailed in the society as girls and boys of all sections of the society participated with equal status.

Chapter VIII

HUNCHARI

Hunchari is the most systematic and disciplined programme of Bohag Bihu in which Bihunach and Bihunam are performed with Bihubadhya. It is not only a programme of entertainment, but also of spiritual importance. In original format, it was performed by a group of menfolk. This group is called as Hunchari-dal. Generally one Hunchari-dal is formed per village except in case of very big village. Additionally, kids organise separate Huchari-dal, and perform in the courtyards families in daytime. Hunchari can be described as of 4 components or parts: Mangaldhani, Hunchari –diha, Bihu and Ashirbad.

Mangaldhani is the foremost part of Hunchari. At the very onset of entering into the courtyard of a family, the Hunchari-dal ushers definite spiritual hymn, and there by worship the God(s) to bless the family with all round prosperity. The head or another member of a family then welcomes Hunchari-dal by following definite rituals.

Hunchari-diha is the second part of the programme in which a Hunchari-dal sings a specific type of Bihunam in definite rhythm different from the rhythm of singing general Bihunam. This very type of Bihunam is called Hunchari-diha or Hunchari-ghokha. In Hunchari-diha, the Hunchari-dal performs a definite type of Bihunach by moving together in circle with definite steps. The subject-matters of the Bihunam sung as Hunchari-diha are generally related to culture, festival, mythological stories, and historical events. Verses of holy books of Ekasharan Dharma namely Kirtan and Namghokha are also sporadically used by a few Hunchari-dal of few villages. At the end of the Hunchari-diha part, generally Khnora-cheu or Nachani-cheu is played in which a few Bihuwa perform Bihunach in general style.

The third part of Hunchari is called as Bihu. It is the most extensive and entertaining component of Hunchari. Bihunam of various subject-matters are sung in this part. Various Dholar-cheu and various types of Bihunach and Bihunam are also presented in this part. Mohor-xingar-penpa is played with great importance. Haat-toka and Pati-tal are used as accompanied Bihubadhya. Some of the Hunchari-dal of some villages also played Baanhi, Gogana, Xutuli, Been and Mitong.

Ashirbad is the last part of Hunchari. The word Ashirbad means blessings. After completion of the Bihu part, the family offers reverence to the Hunchari-dal in definite traditional norms. It is called as Hunchari-Xorai. A Guwapan, some money and preferably a Bihuwan or Seleng-sadar are offered in a Xorai or Bota or Agoli-kolpat as Hunchari-Xorai. The family members then take Xewa to the Hunchari-dal with auspicious spirit. The Hunchari-dal bestowed blessings to the family by ushering spiritual hymns. Then the Hunchari-dal collects the offerings, and returns the Xorai or Bota to the family.

Generally one Hunchari-dal is formed in a village, and performs Hunchari at the courtyards of each of the families of the village. The associated social norm is that every family of a village should get blessings from the village's Hunchari-dal at its courtyard. The blessing of Hunchari-dal is considered as auspicious and essential by each family.

The duration of performing Hunchari in courtyard of a family varies from few minutes to couple of hours depending mostly on willingness of the family, and time available with Hunchari-dal to cover all the families of the village. Based on these two factors, the Bihu part is tailored or skipped off. In case of performing Hunchari in courtyard of a family for couple of hours, the family generally offer considerable amount of money in the Hunchari-Xorai. Some families also entertain the Hunchari-dal with Tea, Pitha, Laru and/or Jalpan or a feast.

As per investigative studies, till early part of the decade of sixties of 20th century, Hunchari was performed only by menfolk in the villages.

The subject-matters of Bihunam of this format of Hunchari are not romantic – not regarding love between boys and girls. Bihunam on various subject-matters such as nature, culture, occupations, social issues, heritage, historical, and mythological are sung in this format. Comedy type of Bihunam and amusing type of Bihunach are of special interesting constituents. Some of the Bihunam of Hunchari of this format express love and respects to relatives including mother, grandmother, aunt, uncle, brother, friends etc.

In the mid part of the decade of sixties of 20th century, in a few villages an additional item added into the event of Hunchari of menfolk. This addition changed the original format of Hunchari to a great extent in subsequent decades and till today. In the newly developed format of Hunchari, one to three numbers of boys of a Hunchari-dal dressed up just like girls, and performed Bihunach as like as girls dance in Rati Bihu and Gastolar Bihu. A boy dresses and dance in Hunchari like a girl was called as Xajowa-nachani in some of the villages. In this format of Hunchari the majority of the Bihunam of the Bihu part became romantic, and the Bihunam on other subject matters became strikingly less. Comedy type of Bihunam and amusing Bihunach also became too less.

Within a span of few years, many villages adopted the new format of Hunchari. Furthermore, after a couple of decades, in some villages girls started participating in the Bihu part of Hunchari, and thus, replaced Xajowa-nachani. Even so, the original format of Hunchari in which only menfolk participate has remained intact in some of the villages. At present, mostly the new format of Hunchari with participation of both males and females is presented in the cultural functions organised at the occasion of Bohag Bihu. Most of the YouTube videos on Hunchari are also of the new format.

Chapter IX

ARCHETYPAL FEATURES OF BIHUNAM

The prototypical songs of Rati Bihu, Jeng Bihu and Hunchari are called as Bihunam. The word Bihugeet is a synonym of Bihunam. Several thousand Bihunam have been composed so far primarily through these three programmes across centuries. These three programmes were held every year in thousands of villages for many centuries, and new Bihunam in terms of lyrics and tunes were added to old ones every year. Of-course, Bihunam are also composed and sung in other situations and occasions too. Till now, more than 5000 Bihunam have so far been documented in print form. Quite obviously, many of the Bihunam composed and sung throughout the centuries are yet to be documented, and many of them might have lost. About hundred different tunes of singing Bihunam have so far become evergreen. This chapter presents the following four aspects of Bihunam:

1. Subject-matters of Bihunam

2. Composition of Bihunam

3. Archetypal ways of singing Bihunam

4. The Rhythms of singing Bihunam

Subject-matters of Bihunam

There are Bihunam of all the subject-matters relating to culture, livelihood, society, heritage, history, mythology, love and emotions of Assamese people, particularly of agrarian Assamese society. All different kinds of feelings and emotions of the agrarian Assamese life are reflected in the Bihunam.

Majority of the Bihunam are of course love songs, and some of them are sensual too. Moreover, there are Bihunam on all different aspects and elements of the rich natural environment of the land Assam. There are many Bihunam which elucidate natural beauty and richness of the nature particularly that of the spring season. There are Bihunam in which specific birds, animals, fish, trees, herbs, rivers, streams, ponds, villages, townships, implements, cosmetics are being referred. Moreover, there are many Bihu nam which express admiration, love and pride relating culture, life-style, historical events, legacy, social-heroes, talents, outstanding performance and the like. There are also Bihunam which describe various items, activities and issues relating to Assamese agrarian society. Many of the Bihunam are pleasantry as well as of comic taste too. There are also Bihunam which reveal traditional wisdoms, social norms and spiritual perspectives. There are Bihunam that delineate interesting stories and events of various mythological, historical and contemporary topics. Regarding the enormous diversity and vastness of the subject matters of Bihunam, a highly acclaimed Assamese author and lyricist of 20th century, Hemanga Biswas stated that whatever is not found in Bihunam – is not exist in Assam.

Bihunam as love-songs

Love is at the core of majority of Bihunam. There are Bihunam of all different types of love. The ancient Greek philosophers classified love into 7 types.[26] There are Bihunam of all these 7 types of love excepting the Storge type. The seven types of love are:

- ➢ Eros love

- ➢ Philia love

- ➢ Agape love

- ➢ Ludus love

- ➢ Pragmam love

- ➢ Philautia love

- ➢ Storge love

Eros type love is the love in the sense of passionate desire for an object, typically sexual passion. This type of love illustrates sexual attraction, bodily beauty, physical desire towards others, and is powerfully passionate. There are - hundreds of Bihunam which reveal intense passion for attaining love of loved one; hundreds of Bihunam which reveal expression of beauty of loved ones; hundreds of Bihunam which reveal physical desire; hundreds of Bihunam which reveal deep sadness as well as frustration related to love; and hundreds of Bihunam which reveal intense restlessness for meeting loved ones. In fact, majority of the Bihunam so far composed reveal Eros type of love. Another point to ponder is that in most of the Bihunam of this type, love is expressed implicitly with superb lyrical standard and brilliant metaphors. Majority of the Bihunam of Rati Bihu reveal this Eros type of love.

Philia love refers to the type of love that one feels for parents, siblings, family members, relatives, companions, and friends. This type of love is linked with loyalty, companionship, and trust. Several dozens of Bihunam have so far been composed that express this type of love. There are Bihunam which reveal love for mother, grandmother, father, uncle, aunt, brother, sister and relatives. There are also Bihunam which reveal companionship to fellow participant. Such Bihunam are sung in Hunchari, and were presented in original format of Hunchari of menfolk with great importance.

Agape love is representative of universal love. It encompasses the kinds of love that people feel for nature, for other humans, for the race, for the country, for the legacy and for the God. There are Bihunam which reveal love for various elements of the nature including birds, river, streams, animals, plants, crops etc. There are Bihunam which reveal love for various tools and implements relating to agriculture and livelihood of Assamese agrarian society. There are Bihunam in which love is expressed for other human is expressed. There are also Bihunam that reveal love for the God. Bihunam of agape love are mainly sung in Jeng Bihu and Hunchari while less in Rati Bihu.

Ludus love refers to flirtatiousness, seduction, and sex without commitment, and is associated with play, teasing, and excitement. Several Bihunam are regarding this type of love. Such Bihunam were sung in Rati Bihu, and also in open fields by cowherds, but not in Jeng Bihu and Hunchari.

Pragma type of love means long-lasting love. In many of the Bihunam inclination for this type of love is expressed. Such Bihunam were sung particularly in Rati Bihu and also to some extent in Jeng Bihu and in the format of Hunchari in which girls also participate.

Philautia represents self-love, self-confidence, self-worth on one hand, and unhealthy and narcissistic feeling and arrogance on the other. There are few Bihunam sang in Rati Bihu which represent this type of love. A few Bihunam of this type of love are also sung in the format of Hunchari in which girls also participate.

Composition of Bihunam

The composition of most of the Bihunam is of Dulari-Chanda. 'Sanskrit prosody or Chandas refers to one of the six Vedangas, or limbs of Vedic studies. This auxiliary discipline has focussed on the poetic metres, including those based on fixed number of syllables per verse, and those based on fixed number of morae per verse".[27] Dulari is one of the types of Chandas. A verse of Dulari-Chanda is combination of two rhythmic verses, and each of the verses is of two lines. Majority of the Bihunam are verses of this type. Thus such a Bihunam can well be considered as a rhyme of total four lines that express a particular meaning. Use of metaphors is one of the distinguishing features of the Bihunam of Dulari-Chanda. In other words, most of the Bihunam of Dulari-Chanda are such that the first two lines express a metaphor corresponding to the message of the next two lines.

There is of course another type of Bihunam which cannot be categorised as of any of the Chandas, and they are used as Jat in the way of singing Bihunam as Jatnam. Nearly one thousand Bihunam of this type have so far been documented in printed form.

Lyrical qualities of Bihunam are of superb standard in terms of all different lyrical characteristics including selective use of words, metaphors, songlike attribute, emotions and personal feelings.

Styles of singing Bihunam

The styles of singing Bihunam are broadly of two types: on rhythmic beats and without rhythmic beats. When a verse of Bihunam is sung without rhythmic beats, it is called as Yojona. Of course, its use is sporadic. The styles singing Bihunam on rhythmic beats are of four types as hereunder:

1. Singing several verses in clusters

It is the style of singing in which a cluster of selected verses of Bihunam of Dulari-Chanda are sung continually one after another by maintaining a rhythm. This was the main way of singing Bihunam in Rati Bihu and Jeng Bihu.

2. Jatnam

It is the style of singing Bihunam in which several rounds of a selected piece of Bihunam called Jat is sung. In each round, one or a part of a verse of Bihunam of Dulari-Chanda is sung with the Jat. This style of singing Bihunam is thus resembles the style of singing Harinam of Vaishnavite religion propagated by Mahapurush Srimanta Sankardeva. A Jat may or may not be of Dulari-Chanda, and may be of several lines or simply a couple of words. Bihunam are sung mostly in this style in Hunchari. Of course, it was also applied in Rati Bihu and Jeng Bihu.

3. Joranam

This style of singing Bihunam was basically followed in Rati Bihu. In this way of singing Bihunam pair of a girl and boy as well as lovers expressed romantic feelings and love to each other and also answer each other's questions by means of Bihunam. The Assamese word jora means pair and nam here refers to Bihunam. Generally a series of Bihunam of Dulari-Chanda are sung as Joranam while the style of Jatnam was also followed to some extent.

This style of singing Bihunam was followed in Rati Bihu. Different pairs of boy and girl as well as lovers sang Joranam in Rati Bihu at different points of time. The Joranam in Rati Bihu covered several purposes relating to love and romance of the participating boys and girls:

- Proposing love to someone for the first time
- Exchange messages regarding love affairs.
- Inviting each other to join hands on certain action
- Planning to overcome hurdles from parents and society for continuing love.
- Expressing disappointments relating to certain actions of either party.
- Awaking regarding certain issue related love affairs
- Deciding to start married life.

The impact of Joranam of Rati Bihu was so intense that there were cases in which lovers decided and gave consent to be life partner by way of singing Joranam. Lovers even sometimes go for married life directly from the Bihukhola. This very style of singing Bihunam is also showcased in the format of Hunchari in which girls also participate.

4. Malita (Ballard)

It is another form of singing and composing Bihunam. A Malita is the combination of several verses that together tell a story or describe an interesting event. The verses of a Malita may or may be of Dulari-Chanda, or combination of both the types of compositions. Such Bihunam are sung in all the three traditional programmes - Rati Bihu, Jeng Bihu and Hunchari.

Rhythms of singing Bihunam

Bihunam are generally sung in a particular rhythm popularly called as Duchaparia-chapari - means two consecutive claps of hands [28]. In Rati Bihu and Jeng Bihu all the Bihunam were sung in the rhythm of Duchaparia-chapari. In Hunchari too Bihunam are mostly sung in this rhythm. The very rhythm of Duchaparia-Chapari is therefore recognized as the marked rhythm of singing Bihunam. The rhythm of Duchaparia-Chapari when played in Bihu-dhol is composed with either all closed *bols* or the last *bol* as closed *bol* – as shown hereunder:

I khit khitI I khit khitI

OR

I khit khitiI I khit taakI

The very rhythm of Duchaparia-Chapari resembles to Khemta Taala of Hindustani music but not the same – definitely different. The Khemta Taala is of 4 Matra while the typical rhythm of singing Bihunam is of 3.5 Matra[29]. This is because the last *bol* or all the *bols* of the rhythm of singing Bihunam are closed *bols*. Noteworthy that the very *bol* produced in playing Toka is very much closed *bol*, and in Rati Bihu and Jeng Bihu the girls sang Bihunam by playing only Toka along with claps to keep rhythm.

Thus, the *"I tok tokI tok tokI"* is the most original rhythm of singing Bihunam. In Hunchari, the Bihunam of Hunchari-diha, Budha-cheu, Hurali-cheu and Kanhi-ghurua-cheu are sung in four different rhythms.

None of the rhythms of singing Bihunam is exactly the same with any of the rhythm or Taala of Hindustani music. The rhythmic difference is the most vivid distinguishing parameter of Bihunam, and based on rhythm, Bihunam can well be distinguished from any other folk songs, modern songs, and classical songs.

Chapter X

PROTOTYPICAL FEATURES OF BIHUNACH

The prototypical features of Bihunach are presented hereunder in following 2 heads:

1. Basic features of Bihunach

2. Men's additional Bihunach in Hunchari

Basic features of Bihunach

Bihu nach is distinctively prototypical dance form of Bohag Bihu festival as well as of Assamese culture from all the following basic parameters.

a. Archetypal rhythm

b. Archetypal movements

c. Archetypal twisting of waist

d. Archetypal poses

e. Archetypal expressions

These parameters are by and large applicable to Bihunach of both females and males. However, Bihunach of female and male are very well distinguishing. Moreover, all these parameters are not applicable to the Bihunach performed by men in Hunchari-diha, Budha-cheu, Hurali-cheu and Kanhi-guruwa-cheu of Hunchari. Therefore, Bihunach of menfolk on these types of Dholar-cheu are presented under a separate heading.

Archetypal rhythm of Bihunach

Bihunach is performed in the same typical rhythm stated in case of Bihunam. It is of Duchaporia-Chapori – Taala of 3.5 Matra's which is composed of all closed *bols* or last *bol* as closed *bol*. Basically this very typical rhythm makes Bihunach prototypical and distinguishing from all other folk dances, classical dances and modern dances.

The original sources of females' Bihunach are Rati Bihu and Jeng Bihu. In Rati Bihu and Jeng Bihu, the girls performed Bihunach by playing Toka, the rhythm of which was "*I tok tokI tok tokI*". As said earlier, the *bol* of Toka is '*tok*' and it is absolutely closed *bol* and thus all the *bols* of the rhythm were closed *bols*. Moreover, the girls also performed Bihunach in Mohor-xingar-penpa played by the boy's group in Rati-bihu, and it was also played in the same rhythm. Hence, Bihunach can be performed in its most precision with Toka, Mohor-xingar-penpa and with Bihunam sung in the rhythm of Duchaporia-Chapori. In new format of Hunchari, the Xojowa-nachani as well as girls therefore generally did not perform Bihunach in Dholar-cheu except in case of Kanhi-guruwa-cheu.

In present era, the girls perform Bihunach in Dholar-cheu too. The artists of new generations have also constructed a few new Dholar-cheu or *bajna* especially suitable for performing Bihunach by Bihuwati.

Archetypal movements of Bihunach

Bihunach is performed in small steps along with rolling toes on floor in typical ways, and by maintaining the typical rhythm. Also make movement at intervals by whirling body.

Archetypal twisting of waist in Bihunach

In Bihunach performers twist waist almost intermittently by maintaining the typical rhythm. Generally they twist waist twice in the typical rhythm of 3.5 Matra.

Typical expressions of Bihunach

Bihunach expresses both outer and inner beauty of performer. Poses of Bihunach do not symbolize anything specifically. In Bihunach performer expresses joy, love, delight, exhilaration, thrill and the like. Moreover, performer keeps smile throughout the performance. Natural smile and natural expression of joy in the face particularly in eyes and lips is another worth mentioning feature of Bihunach. Another basic feature is that none of the Bhangima (poses) of Bihunach depicts any meaning directly as well as vividly. In other words, they were not composed to express certain meaning. And that is a unique difference of Bihunach from some other forms of folk dance and from classical dances such as Satria nitya, Bharat Natyam, Kuchipudi etc.

Of course, in present era, one style of Bihunach has been added from a traditional dance of Mising community of Assam in which different activities related to cultivation of *Sali*-paddy, and processing of its harvest are shown. The protectionists of Bihu -culture as well as 'Bihu Surashya Sommitty, Assam' do not recognize this style as of prototypical Bihunach.

Archetypal poses (Bhangima) of Bihunach

As because Rati Bihu and Jeng Bihu were held in midst of nature, and girls danced spontaneously, there was no definite poses of girls' Bihunach. However, in modern era, Bihunach is showcased in the cultural functions arranged at the occasion of Bohag Bihu and also in various cultural events held outside the state and abroad. Moreover, competitions of Bihunach in various forms are also held. In this context, researchers and social activists in the field have identified the prototypical poses of Bihunach so that they are performed by maintaining the archetypical features. A dance pose is called as Bhangima in Assamese.

The 'Bihu Surashya Sommitty, Assam', the organization working for protecting, preserving and spreading of Bihu-culture in its original form and features has recognized 8 types of Bhangima of

Bihuwati's Bihunach.[30] The Bihuwa perform three of these 8 types of Bhangmia. The photographs of these 8 types of Bhangmia are presented in Appendix VI.

Bihuwa's structured Bihunach in Hunchari

Bihuwa perform Bihunach basically in Hunchari, and their Bihunach is specific to different kinds of Dholar-cheu. In Khnora-cheu, Nachani-cheu and Digholiya-cheu and also in Cheus of Mohor-xingar-penpa they perform Bihunach by following the already stated basic features of Bihunach. On the other hand, in case of Hunchari-diha, Burda-cheu, Hurali-cheu, Dutiya-cheu, and Kanhi-guruwa-cheu Bihuwa perform definitely structured Bihunach. The movements of feet and types of Bhangmia are definite in the Bihunach performed in each of these four types of Dholar-cheu. The standard of composition, nature, style and standard of these Bihunach are close to that of classical dances such as Satriya Nritya, Bharat natayam and Kuchipudi.

As stated earlier, Burda-cheu is comprised of total 13 numbers of bajnas which include one Mul-bajna and twelve Xanchar. The Hunchari-dal performs definitely structured sets of Bihunach in each of these 13 numbers of *bajna*. All the Bihuwa of Hunchari-dal take part and perform the Bihunach synchronously. Similarly, Hurali-cheu is comprised of 6 different *bajna* of Bihu-dhol. All members of Hunchari-dal perform definitely structured set of Bihunach in each of these 6 *bajna* by moving in a circle. In Dutia-cheu two Bihuwa of Hunchari-dal perform quite distinctive and amusing kind of Bihunach. In Kanhi-ghurua-cheu, Bihunach is presented by using dishes of bell-metal as prop. The movements of feet and types of Bhangmia are definite and distinctive. Traditionally, Assamese people use dishes and bowls of bell-metal as utensils, and they are considered as symbol of prestige.

Even in the format of Hunchari in which Bihuwati participate, the structured sets of Bihunach of Hunchari-diha, Burda-cheu, Hurali cheu and Dutia-cheu are performed only by the Bihuwa. On the other hand, the Bihuwati perform Bihunach in Kanhi-ghuruwa-cheu in the new format of Hunchari.

Chapter XI

COSTUMES AND ORNAMENTS OF BIHUNACH

As because Rati Bihu and Jeng Bihu were originally held in midst of nature and both the events were meant for self-entertainment of the participants, so, costume and ornaments were not definite. The girls and boys went to participate in the programmes with costumes according to their choices. Of-course, girls preferred to wear flowers at hairs.

On the other hand, as Hunchari is performed in courtyards of the families, and so, audience are there to enjoy the programme. Even so, costumes are not definite but a few dress codes are followed spontaneously.

In context to Bihu-competitions, guidelines on costumes and ornaments have been prescribed. These are also by and large followed in other kinds of theatrical performances of Bihunach, Bihunam and Bihubadhya. Heritages of Assamese culture and relevant facts of various dimensions have been taken into consideration in formulating these guidelines. The costumes and ornaments prescribed in the set of guidelines of 'Bihu Surashya Sommitty, Assam' are presented below in two heads.[30] Photographs of Assamese ornaments are presented in Appendix IX.

Costumes and ornaments of Bihuwati

Several clauses regarding costumes and ornaments of Bihuwati have been specified in the above mentioned guidelines of Bihu-competitions. Major points of selected clauses are briefly presented below.

1. The main costumes of Bihuwati are Riha, Mekhela and Blouse. Riha and Mekhela are two kinds of typical traditional Assamese dress wear by women not only for performing Bihunach but also in other occasions. At present, Assamese women wear Sadar, Mekhela and Blouse in day to day life. Riha is similar to Sadar but not exactly the same.

2. The blouse of Bihuwati should cover back of the body adequately, and up-to waist. The sleeves of blouse should ideally be up-to the elbow.

3. The Riha, Mekhela and Blouse may be of Muga colour or of pure Muga fabric. Black colour cotton Mekhela and red or black blouse also mentioned as acceptable in the set of guidelines. It is worth mentioning in this context that Muga silk is regarded as a pride of Assam. It is one of the finest and most valuable silk in the globe. The fabric is remarkably durable and matchlessly beautiful with golden colour and glossy texture. The fabric as well as costumes of Muga silk last for generations with same quality of colour and texture. Muga silkworm, Antheraea assmensism (Helfer) is endemic to NE India particularly to Assam, and it is still exists in a different parts of the region. Muga based sericulture is Age-old tradition of Assamese culture, and Assam is the largest producer of Muga silk in the world.

4. The floral patterns of Riha, Mekhela and Blouse should represent rich Assamese tradition. Weaving is superbly rich and glorious tradition of Assamese women. They traditionally create wonderful and splendid typical floral patterns by weaving. Weaving of Bihuwan for Bohag Bihu is traditionally recognised as customary.

5. Bihuwati may add a Hanchati near the waist. Hanchati is a typical traditional handkerchief used by Assamese women.

6. Bihuwati should preferably adorn hair with typical Assamese flowers particularly, Kopouphul, Togorphul and Naharphul.

7. Bihuwati should wear Assamese traditional ornaments. There are varieties of Assamese traditional jewelleries of enchanting designs. The traditional jewellery designs contain motifs of flora and fauna and Assamese traditional musical instruments. The Assamese jewelleries of Assamese women include:

> Thuria

> Golpota

> Gejera

> Junbiri

> Dholbiri

> Gumkharu

> Muthikharu

> Dugdugi

> Bena

> Rongamoni

> Xilikhamoni

> Kerumoni

> Zangfai keru

> Saratia

Assamese jewelleries are traditionally crafted with hands by skilled Assamese artisans. The craft of Assamese jewelleries including gold-washing and manufacturing gold ornaments is an age old tradition in Assam. 'Manufacture of gold ornaments, as well as gold washing flourished in mediaeval Assam during the Ahom dynasty. Gold-dust was found abundantly in Subonsiri one of tributaries of the Brahmaputra. Jorhat and Sonari in Upper Assam, Nagoan in central Assam and Borpeta in lower Assam have been the major hubs of manufacturing Assamese jewelleries throughout the ages'.[31] At present, several production units and shops of Assamese traditional jewelleries are there throughout the state. Assamese women have been continuing wearing mainly the amazing Assamese traditional jewelleries.

Costumes of Bihuwa

As prescribed in the said guidelines, the costumes of Bihuwa include Dhuti, Shirt of traditional style, Bihuwan and Tongali. Bihuwa does not wear any ornament.

Chapter XII

EVOLUTION OF BIHU FESTIVALS

The Assamese race has been celebrating Bihu festivals from pre-historic era. Therefore, the epoch of its commencement cannot be ascertained precisely. However, its evolution since pre-historic period to till date can be delineated based on relevant historical information and evidential facts. For this purpose, at the outset we need to reflect on the timeline regarding different races lived in Assam since pre-historic era, and also on the ethnic composition of the Assamese race. It is also necessary to ponder on major political, socio-cultural, educational and technological influences on Assamese race across the centuries. Keeping all these in view, this chapter is organised under the following heads:

1. Ethnic diversity in Assam

2. Evolution of Assamese language

3. Influence of Ekasarana Dharma

4. Influence of colonial period

5. Influence of post independent period

6. Evolution of modern cultural functions of Bohag Bihu

7. Evolution of Guidelines of Bihu-competitions

Ethnic diversity in Assam

The anthropological studies ascertain that Austroasiatic as well as Austroasiatic language speaking people were the earliest aboriginal people lived in Assam. They lived in Brahmaputra valley for about two thousand year, and then migrated to Meghalaya and Bangladesh. Then after immigration of several ethnic races as well as groups to the land Assam took place till the present era. "The peopling of Assam was first started with a wave of migration of the Australoids or Austro-Asiatic speaking people from south-east Asia…The second group to have come to Assam from the north-east and east are the people speaking Tibeto-Burman languages, especially eastern Himalayan, north Assam, Bodo and Naga groups of languages. These are racially Mongoloid people and unlike the Austro-Asiatic, they set up a stream of migration which has been continuing till today. ... Almost at the same time as the Tibeto-Burman, or perhaps a bit later, there started another stream of migration of the people speaking Indo-Aryan languages from the plains of northern India, perhaps during the first millennium B.C. The fourth streams of new arrivals were Muslim personnel of the army of Muhammad-i-Bakhtiyar left back after his disastrous Tibet expeditions. The fifth wave of immigrants was Tai Shan People, who entered Assam under the leadership of Sukaphaa from Hukawng Valley in Myanmar via Pangsau Pass in 1228 and settled between Buridihing and Dikhou rivers. The sixth stream of peoples between the 17th and 19th centuries, were Tai - Buddhists. The seventh wave of people into Assam occurred soon after the beginning the colonial period in Assam after the First Anglo-Burmese War and the Treaty of Yandaboo in 1826—the political instability led to the immigration of Kachin and Kuki people from Upper Burma into Assam across the Patkai and Arakan Yoma. Following the establishment of the tea industry in Assam, and after the companies failed in harnessing the labour of the local Kachari, people from the Chotanagpur area of Bihar, northern and western Orissa, eastern Madhya Pradesh, and northern Andhra Pradesh belonging to Munda, Ho, Santal, Savara, Oraon, Gond and other ethnic groups were recruited for labour in the newly emerging tea estates. British colonialism opened the borders of Assam, hitherto controlled tightly by the Ahom and Dimasa kingdoms, and established a new order causing a significant influx from Bengal, Rajasthan, North India and Nepal".[32] The Dravidians might be a branch of Indo-Aryans who came to Assam during the first millennium BC.[33] Lastly, immigration of Muslim and Hindu Bengali population took place from East-Pakistan as well as Bangladesh.

"The bulk of population of the Brahmaputra valley is comprised of tribes whose peculiar dialects belong to the Tibeto-Burman branch of the Indo-Chinese family by no means indicates racial uniformity. All that it can fairly be held to show is that the most recent conquerors prior to Ahom, were speakers of such dialects, and that they imposed their language on older inhabitants, whose identity gradually became merged in that of their conquerors." [34]

The Yogis being the followers of a particular religious sect, formed into a caste after the decline of the later form of Buddhism about 12th - 13th century A. D. During the Ahom rule the Yogis were registered into grid called khel, and assigned the duty of rearing mulberry silk and spinning its thread. They were therefore called Katani.[35]

Thus, the Assamese race is comprises of a wide range of ethnic groups mainly of Tibeto-Burman, Tai-Ahom, Indo-Aryan, Alpine-Aryan, Kuki-chin, Dravidian, Muslim, Bengali, and Tea garden labourers. Resultantly, at present the people of Assam are not only multi-ethnic but also of multi-linguistic and multi-religious. There are more than hundred castes of people presently living in Assam. Some of the ethnic groups have been adopting own ethnic languages, though majority of the people of Assamese race speak Assamese language. Thus, in terms of all different socio-cultural aspects, the culture of the people of Assam is intermixed of the cultures of diverse ethnic groups. Moreover, there are influences of the culture of Austroasiatic people who originally lived in this land for more than thousands of years, and also intermixed and assimilated with Tibeto-Burman people to considerable extent.

Evolution of Assamese language

"Assamese is an Indo-Aryan language spoken mainly in the northeast Indian state of Assam, where it is an official language. It is the easternmost Indo-European language".[36] It "serves almost as a lingua franca among the different speech communities in the whole area. The earliest literary work available which may be claimed as distinctly Asamiya is the Prahrada Carita written by a court poet named Hema Sarasvati in the latter half of the thirteenth century AD".[37] "The language moved to the court of the Ahom kingdom in the seventeenth century".[38] As because, Ahom kingdom ruled almost entire Brahmaputra valley for nearly 600 years, being the court language the Assamese language worked as a strong catalyst for intermixing and alliance of various ethnic groups of the land. At present, majority of the people of Brahmaputra valley of Assam speak Assamese language. Of course, some of the ethnic groups are continuing their original ethnic languages as mother tongue. Assamese language is one of the main parameters for identity of Assamese people or Assamese race.

On the other hand, some of the ethnic groups have been celebrating agrarian folk festivals similar to the Bihu festivals but in specific names of own ethnic languages and with ethnically typical rituals, dance, music of own culture. Nevertheless, a couple of these ethnic groups also celebrate the three Bihu festivals additionally.

Influence of Ekasarana Dharma

The propagation of Ekasarana Dharma, a neo-Vaishanavite religion by the genius Assamese polymath Srimanta **Sankardeva (1449-1568) played most significant role in integration of various ethnic groups of Assam as Assamese race. The** multifaceted intellect, Srimanta **Sankardeva being a super brilliant** saint-scholar, poet, playwright, and socio-religious reformer contributed immensely in all aspects of life of the people of Assam across the ethnic groups. Ekasarana Dharma was spread through Assamese language, and holy books of the religion were written in Assamese language. So, this very religion encompassed people across the ethnic originality in term of religious perspectives and Assamese language. Thus spread of Ekasarana Dharma played a vital role in evolution and growth of Assamese race too, and therefore, Srimanta **Sankardeva is regarded as father of modern Assamese race.**

Quite obviously, Ekasarana Dharma contributed substantial and sustainable impact on the Bihu festivals. In most of the villages, the rituals of the Bihu festivals particularly the religious one became oriented upon the norms and rituals of this religion. The influences are distinctive in case of Hunchari too. In most of the villages, the Mangaldhani and Ashirbad parts of Hunchari became according to Ekasarana Dharma. Moreover, it can well be postulated that the Hunchari-diha of Hunchari might has evolved as a result of inspiration of the style of singing Ghokha-Pod of Ekasarana Dharma. Same point is applicable in case of the style of singing Jatnam in Hunchari. As said earlier, Hunchari-diha and Jatnam are sung in the style of singing Ghokha-Pod in Ekasarana Dharma. Moreover, selected verses of the holy book Kirtan of Ekasarana Dharma are also sporadically used as Hunchari-diha. Furthermore, singing of mythological verses as Hunchari-diha and as Bihunam of Burda-cheu and Hurali-cheu is another influence of Ekasarana Dharma on Hunchari.

Influence of colonial period

As a result of the peace treaty known as Treaty of Yandabo signed at the end of the First Anglo Burmese War in the year1826, the state of Assam was annexed with British ruled India. The British rule continued till India achieved independence in year 1947. During this colonial period particularly in last decades of 19th century Rati Bihu and Jeng Bihu encountered serious hindrance. A few of the Assamese educated and affluent personalities started campaigning against these programmes of Bohag Bihu. They perceived that the Bihunam and Bihunach of Rati Bihu and Jeng Bihu are erotic in nature, and hence, continuation of the same by holding the programmes in midst of nature would downgrade the image of Assamese race in modern society. Moreover, they perceived that continuation of such programmes as part of Bohag Bihu would be disadvantageous for modern development of Assamese people. They therefore tried to disseminate their perceptions among the contemporary educated and wealthy class of Assamese people.

The great Vietnamese Buddhist monk, Thich Nhat Hanth said 'People deal too much with the negative, with what is wrong. Why not try and see positive things, to just touch those things and make them bloom'. Fortunately, there were several highly educated and intellectual Assamese personalities at that point of time who looked at Rati Bihu and Jeng Bihu positively. They regarded these programmes as glorious heritage of the race, and could emphasise how deeply the agrarian Assamese society love Bihunach, Bihunam, Rati Bihu and Jeng Bihu. They also possessed deep realisms – how auspiciously both the programmes are organised - how strictly the discipline, norms and ethics are maintained. Among this very group there were several all-time great Assamese personalities, authors and artists. The top most of them are - Rupkonwar Jyoti Prasad Agarwala, Sahityarathi Lakshminath Bezborua, Padmanath Gohain Boruah, Sarat Chandra Goswami, Rajani Kanta Bordoloi, Hemanga Biswas and Bolinarayan Bora.[39] This august group boldly opposed the anti-group, and expressed and spread their views widely in several ways.

American author Eric Hoffer in his famous book 'The Passionate State of Mind: And Other Aphorisms' writes - "Rudeness is the weak man's imitation of strength'.[40] The anti-group kept up their antipathy and revulsion, and took rather rude approach to stop Rati Bihu and Jeng Bihu. A few writers of that group elucidated these two programmes from negative perspectives in a few books and magazines which include, Asom Buranji, Arunodoi, Jonaki, Assam Bondhu and The National Guardian.[41]

Moreover, the anti-group became quite active to convince some of the Bengali officials working in Assam in key positions in the British government. Finally, by following set official procedure, the anti-group submitted written application to the British Government to officially ban Rati Bihu and Jeng Bihu. As a result, in the early part of 1899, the British government issued an ordinance to ban programmes like Rati Bihu and Jeng Bihu. The Assamese people by and large, particularly the agrarian people and also the aforesaid educated section socked for the imposed ban. They expressed their views at their levels. Moreover, one person Moimat Tatinga Bora from a village of Nagoan district filed a case at Guwahati High Court against the ordinance. He filed the case through a person of his village namely Ananda Das who was an employee in the court. At that point of time the judge of the case in the court was Fatik Chandra Boruah of Puronigudam of Nagaon district. The court's verdict went in favour of Moimat Tatinga Bora, and resultantly the British government lifted the ban in last part of 1899. Moimat Tatinga Bora became so happy with the judgement that he along with his sister Senimai Bora expressed joy by dancing Bihunach, singing Bihunam, and playing Bihu-dhol instantly in the court. Furthermore, immediately after the verdict, he along with others celebrated the win by arranging a Bihu-function at Puranigudam though the season was not of Bohag Bihu. [42,,43, 44]

Although the official ban on Rati Bihu and Jeng Bihu lifted vide court's verdict, the impacts of the effort of the anti-group sustained among some of the people as well as families. Consequently, Rati Bihu and Jeng Bihu were impaired to a considerable extent. The educated and affluent Assamese people were increasingly influenced by the views of the anti-group, and as a result, started to downplay these programmes and also Bihunach and Bihunam. Many of them grew perception that uneducated and lower socio-economic class only take part in Rati Bihu and Jeng Bihu. Due to these influences, some of the affluent and progressive families in the villages started playing role in restraining their children from participating in these two programmes. It is universally true that educated, affluent and intellectual class directly or indirectly takes the steering of a society and culture. Thus, some of the educated and wealthy families, though fewer in number played considerable role in restricting these two programmes. Of course, the changed political, social and occupational circumstances prevailed as a result of colonial rule were also unfavourable for holding Rati Bihu and Jeng Bihu in midst of nature. Even so, Assamese agrarian society continued these programmes to the maximum possible extent during the colonial period.

Status of Bihu festivals during post-colonial period

The above stated aversion to Rati Bihu and Jeng Bihu sustained after independence of the country too. In fact, it spread to more numbers of socio-economically progressive and affluent families in more villages. The changing educational, occupational, economic and socio-cultural circumstances in the state as well as country also became uncomplimentary for holding these two programmes with same vigour. As a result, within about 3 decades of post-independence, the tradition of holding of Rati Bihu and Jeng Bihu was closed down in most of the villages. At present in no village these programmes are organised in midst of nature.

On the other hand, the Hunchari programme in the courtyards of the families was taken place with full vigour in the villages till last part of 20th century. In those decades wealthy families invited Hunchari-dal of other villages too with the purpose of enjoining the programme along with others of the village, and also to obtain blessings. The Assamese families in the towns of upper Assam also invited Hunchari-dal from their original villages to perform in their courtyards so as to obtain the blessings.

But since dawn of new millennium, the tradition of performing Hunchari in courtyards of families started dwindling. It is mainly due to rising pressure of education on the youths, and occupational diversity of Assamese people living in both rural and urban sectors. Migration of rural youths to urban places within and outside the state is another cause of dwindling trend of Hunchari in last two decades.

Another cause of the dwindling trend of Hunchari in the villages is raising individualism as well as self-centredness in the society. In an article published in 'Psychology Today' in the year 2017, Ronald E Riggio, one of the acclaimed authors in the field of psychology elucidates reasons of the raising self-centredness in modern world in these words: "One trend is that as countries become more economically developed, there tends to be a rise in individualism. More affluence leads to a greater sense of self-reliance and a detachment from others. ... Social media, while it connects us to others, may actually lead to greater self-centredness as people strive to make their presence known".[45] Both the trends are by and large apparently perceptible in case of Assamese people too during post independent period, particularly in new millennium. Abundance and sky high sophistications of electronic and information technologies including TV, mobile, internet are also playing significant role. In the word of internationally acclaimed American author Wendell Berry, "The freedom of affluence opposes and contradicts the freedom of community life". [46]

Evolution of modern day cultural functions

Evolution 'is a creative process, something new appearing at every step of developmental history. Every change is a transformation".[47]

During colonial and post-colonial period, many of the Assamese intellectuals and social activists were keenly observing the dwindling trend of Rati Bihu, Jeng Bihu as well as Bihunach and Bihunam with heavy hearts. Perhaps they could envisage that attempt for restraining Rati Bihu and Jeng Bihu in its original form in the midst of nature might not be a practical proposition in the rapidly changing socio-cultural, educational and economic situations. Hence, they pondered and put effort to explore ways, means and alternatives for sustaining Bihunach, Bihunam and the traditional programmes in the environment of modern era. This resulted in initiation of organising modern era's cultural functions as part of celebrating Bohag Bihu.

At present 1 to 3 days duration cultural events are organised as a part of celebrating Bohag Bihu. Throughout the month of Bohag, several hundreds of such cultural events are organised in knock and corners of the state including both urban and rural localities. These cultural functions are called in several names such as Bihutoli, Bihu-sanmilan, Bihu-utshav, Basanta-mela and Basanta-utsav. As said earlier, in this book the term Bihutoli is used to mean such a function.

The first such Bihutoli was organised in the year 1872 at Gohain goan of Dhemaji district. A stage in the model of Rang-Ghar was constructed with bamboo and timber, and the function was held for 3 days. Since then, this Bihutoli has been organised every year. The people of the village organised 147th years of the Bihutoli in 2019, and planning to organise its 150 years of celebration in 2022. At this juncture, I would like to express sincere thanks to Hari Narayan Borgohain of Jorhat for providing this valuable information with evidential photograph. The trend of organising such Bihutoli however has not spread to other localities of the state in several subsequent decades. In the year 1934, a stage-based Bihutoli was organised at Golaghat, and then after another in 1935 at Dergoan.[48] In the year

1946 such a Bihutoli was organised at Dibrugarh, and then in 1952 at Guwahati in Latashil field.[49]

Then after, the system of organising Bihutoli spread slowly to other places, and thus numbers increased year by year. During the decades of seventies to nineties of 20th century mushroom growth of such Bihutoli took place. The trend ascended upward in new millennium too. Thus, at present several hundreds of Bihutoli are organised throughout the state during the whole month of Bohag. Moreover, similar functions are also organised by Assamese people living in different places outside the state and abroad as part of celebrating Bohag Bihu festival.

Programmes of Bihutoli

Various cultural programmes are held in present day Bihutoli which can broadly be categorised as follows:

1. Bihu-competitions: Competitions of Hunchari, Jeng Bihu, Bihuwati, Bihuwa, Bihunam, Bihunach, Dhol-badan, Penpa-badan, Pitha-pona, Koni-yunj, Assamese traditional dress.

2. Showcasing of Hunchari, Jeng Bihu, Bihunach, Oja dhol-badan.

3. Showcasing of traditional dance and music of ethnic groups of Assam

4. Celebrity artist's programmes on modern Assamese songs and modern Bihugeet with western musical instruments.

Moreover, seminar, lecture, and discussion sessions on selected topics on Bihu-culture are also organised in some Bihutoli.

Types and Programmes of Bihutoli

Based on type of arrangement, the present day Bihutoli can be classified into two categories:

1. Bihutoli with stage

2. Mukoli Bihutoli

Programmes of Bihutoli with stage

In majority of the stage-based Bihutoli two or three types of programmes out of the aforesaid four types are arranged. Of course, in a few of the stage-based Bihutoli all the aforesaid 4 types of programmes are arranged. Such Bihutoli are of big budget.

At present the most widely organised programme in majority of stage-based Bihutoli is - celibrity artist's programmes on modern Assamese songs and modern Bihugeet with western musical instruments. Of course exceptions are there. In quite few stage-based Bihutoli only Bihu-competitions are arranged and rest three types of programmes are not arranged. In a few others Bihutoli of this type all the others 3 types of programmes are arranged except the programmes of celebrity artist on modern Assamese songs and modern Bihugeet with western musical instruments.

Programmes of Mukoli-Bihutoli

Such a Bihutoli is arranged in an open field without theatre stage. In this type of Bihutoli programmes of modern Assamese songs and modern Bihugeet with western musical instruments are not arranged. Out of the rest types of programmes any one or two, or all three types of programmes are arranged. The numbers of Mukoli-Bihutoli are of course quite few - less than 10 per cent of total Bihutoli organised throughout the state. This type of Bihutoli is called as Mukoli-Bihu in short.

Evolution of Guidelines of Bihu-competitions

Bihu-competitions in the Bihutoli were organised somewhat easy-going ways till the decade of seventies of 20th century. Numbers of Bihutoli were also quite less, and the whole affairs of Bihu-competitions in a Bihutoli were subjected to management of the organising committee of the Bihutoli. Till then, there was no widely acceptable set of guidelines to hold the Bihu-competitions. But since last part of the decade of seventies, the number of Bihutoli in the state started increasing substantially. Consequently, organising of Bihu-competitions emerged as quite complex affairs, particularly in relation to judgements on performances of the competitors and selection of best performers. This situation provoked all concerned to work for formulation of detailed guidelines of organising all different types of Bihu-competitions.

As stated earlier, Rati Bihu and Jeng Bihu were held in the midst of nature in many villages for many centuries. In both the programmes, the Bihuwati performed Bihunach spontaneously. So, quite obviously, various features particularly the Bhangima of Bihuwati's Bihunach across the villages were not exactly the same. Moreover, in most of the villages, both Rati Bihu and Jeng Bihu were closed down by end of the decade of sixties of 20th century. In this situation, it was quite challenging for present day researchers to ascertain different types of prototypical Bhangima of Bihuwati's Bihunach. Even so, based on extensive investigative studies as well as interviews of those who participated in the programmes in different villages, several researchers could identify and specify the prototypical features of Bihuwati's Bihunach in terms of rhythms, feet and body movements, poses(Bhangima), twisting of waist and expressions. Fortunately, the researches resulted in consensus among the researchers, practitioners and social activists on these features. Even so, some amount of difference of opinion prevailed regarding Bhangima. According to one school of thought there are total 8 types of archetypical Bhangima of Bihuwati's Bihunach while according to another school of thought there are a few more archetypical

Bhangima. Nonetheless, the research findings and discussion formed a strong base for formulation of guidelines for holding various competitions relating to Bihuwati's Bihunach. On the other hand, all facts and information required for formulation of guidelines for Hunchari competition were readily available as it was prevailing with all vigour.

Based on the research findings, several cultural organisations at different parts of state organised workshops and conferences which resulted in formulation of detailed guidelines on different Bihu-competitions. However, adoption of different sets of guidelines at different parts of the state was an issue to be resolved. In order to address this issue the 'Bihu Kristi Charcha and Bikash Sommitti, Jorhat organised a state level workshop at Jorhat in the year 1981. A considerable numbers of practitioners of Bihu-culture and several prominent researchers, authors, and journalists participated and presented deliberations in the workshop. The workshop was inaugurated by Ananda Mohan Bhagawati and chaired by Khetradhar Borgohain. Among those who contributed significantly include, Porag Chaliha, Joykanta Gandhia, Pradip Neog (author of this book), Kolamoni Handique, Deba Dutta, Bhola Kakoti, Ananda Chandra Dutta, Atul Dutta, Dr. Padmadhar Saikia, Dr. Dulon Knower (President of the Sommitti), Prabir Dutta (General Secretary of the Sommitti), Rabin Rajkhowa, Mallika Rahman, Chitralota Phukon, Amol Rajkhowa, Ashok Bordoloi and Prafulla Rajknowar.[50] The guidelines already formulated through the workshops held earlier at other places were also thoroughly discussed. As aimed at, the workshop resulted in formulation of a set of more detailed guidelines for organising and conducting all different the Bihu-competitions. Soon after this workshop, the 'Bihu Kristi Charcha and Bikash Sommitti, Jorhat' in collaboration with the 'Krixoloi Sanskritik Gosti, Nagoan organised a conference with the purpose of enhancing the acceptability of the set of guidelines throughout the state. Then after, the Sommitti published the set of guidelines in printed form in the year 2005. This set of guidelines was adopted by many of Bihutoli of the state for several decades.

In 2011, the 'Bihu Surashya Sommitty, Assam' prepared and produced a set of all-inclusive guidelines of Bihu-competitions. This set of guidelines was prepared by consulting 12 selected books, 6 sets of already prevailed guidelines of Bihu-competitions, and by organising threadbare discussions among artists, researchers, authors and social activists in the field of Bihu-culture across the state. At present, majority of the Bihutoli of the state and all concerned follow this set of guidelines. 'Bihu Surashya Sommitty, Assam' is also continuing production and distribution of the set of guidelines throughout the state.

Bihu-competitions have been serving pivotal role in preservation and practice of traditional form of Bihunach, Bihunam, Bihubadhya, Jeng Bihu and Hunchari with original prototypical distinctiveness. The guidelines of Bihu-competitions not only encompass procedural aspects but also the prototypical features of Bihunach, Bihunam, Bihubadhya, Bihu -costumes, Jeng Bihu and Hunchari. Thus, the formulation and wide acceptance of the set of guidelines served as total guide for organisers on one hand and for the competitors, judges and all others. Moreover, the guidelines also helped the system of organising Bihu-competitions to gain more vigour and thereby spread throughout the state fast. Furthermore, the Bihu-competitions became the main basis and scope to learn and practice Bihunach, Bihunam, Bihubadhya, Jeng Bihu and Hunchari.

Chapter XIII

IMPACTS OF MODERNIZATION OF BIHU FESTIVALS

As defined in Encyclopedia.com, "Modernization is the current term for an old process—the process of social change whereby less developed societies acquire characteristics common to more developed societies." In present era, impact of modernisation on various traditional cultures has emerged as an important thrust area of research across the globe, because modernization has serious impact on traditional culture including folk music and folk dance all over the world. This point is stressed in a working paper entitled 'Bolivia Tsimane Amazonian Panel Study' in these words: 'Loss of culture of indigenous groups has been central to cultural anthropologists because it represents the irreversible loss of humanity's heritage and diversity.' [51]

Social scientist Thomas Turino in his widely read book , 'Music as a Social Life', stated the significance of folk culture in these words : "Music, dance festivals, and other public expressive cultural practices are primary ways that people articulate the collective identities that are fundamental to forming and sustaining social groups, which are in turn, basic to survival and through music individuals or group can manifest their emotion between themselves and divine to celebrate wedding and to sustain friendship and community and also to inspire mass social and political movements". [52]

Impacts of modernisation on Bihunam, Bihunach, Bihubadhya and Hunchari are quite conspicuous, and are putting serious threat against their safeguarding and preservation of their original distinctiveness. Some of the rituals of the Bihu festivals have also been affected due to modernisation. This chapter presents major issues and concerns of safeguarding and preservation of the intangible heritages of the Bihu festivals. The chapter also highlights the efforts putting towards safeguarding and preservation at organisational and individual level. Various aspects are presented under the following 5 heads:

- ➢ Modernisation of Bihunam
- ➢ Modernisation of Bihunach
- ➢ Impacts of modernisation on Bihutoli
- ➢ Modernisation of Bihu-competitions
- ➢ Impact of modernisation on rituals

Modernisation of Bihunam

The most serious and far-reaching impact of modernisation has occurred in case of Bihunam or Bihugeet. During the decade of eighties of 20th century, the impacts of modernisation on Bihunam became quite discernible. During this decade, considerable numbers of audio cassettes of Bihugeet have been produced by various artists and producers. In a few of the cassettes, several original Bihunam have been presented in original form by maintaining typical rhythm, tunes, and by using only the Bihubadhya. But in other cassettes, the Bihunam have been presented in slightly different form – slightly different rhythm, different style but with typical lyrics and traditional tunes. In other word Bihugeet are presented with flavour of modern songs. Moreover, in such cassettes the Bihugeet have been presented with music created primarily with western musical instruments instead of the prototypical Bihubadya. These songs, though presented as Bihugeet are not recognised precisely as archetypical Bihugeet or Bihunam by the organisations as well as social activists working for safeguarding and preservation of Bihu-culture.

As a result of technology development, the audio cassettes have been replaced by CDs and videos in subsequent decades. In these formats too both the aforesaid categories of Bihugeet have been presented. Thus, since the decade of eighties till now several hundreds of Bihugeet of both the said categories have been presented in the electronic formats. However, the numbers of Bihugeet of precisely original form with traditional Bihubadhya are quite less in electronic format. Furthermore, in electronic mediums, the category of Bihugeet sung with western musical instruments attained overwhelming popularity particularly among the new generation youths. Of course radio has been plating significant role in broadcasting the original form of Bihugeet.

Modernisation on Bihunach

During the decades of seventies and eighties of 20th century several types of Bhangima and movements from a few other forms of Indian dances were entered to Bihuwati's Bihunach through the modern Bihutoli. Some of the artists unnecessarily attempted to enrich Bihunach with kinds of more assortments. As a result, the prototypical distinctiveness of Bihunach was threatened to a great extent. Fortunately, several researchers, authors and social activists of the field including Joykanta Gandhia, Ananda Mohan Bhagawati, Krisna Kanta Handique, Dr. Pradip Neog, Dr. Anil Saikia, Tirtha Phukon, Dinesh Gogoi, Homnath Bora(Oja), Ismail Hussain, Pabitra Mohan Phukan, Durlav Buragohain, Tokheswar Chetia and many others could contribute timely and fight back boldly enough to stop the unwarranted trend, and could expel out the non-typical poses and movements entered into the traditional form of Bihuwati's Bihunach. Those poses were imitations of certain poses of the dance forms such as Satriya Nritya, Bharat Natyam, Kuchipudi and Bhangra. With the purpose of eliminating the unwarranted poses, quite a good numbers of articles published in magazines and newspapers, and many awareness campaigns were held to develop mass awareness on prototypical features of Bihuwati's Bihunach, and to explain why and how those imitated poses are not to be adopted, and how inclusion of those could extinguish the prototypical distinctiveness of Bihunach. As a result, almost all such imitative poses and movements have been expelled from Bihunach within a couple of decades.

Inclusion of new choreographs into Bihuwati's Bihunach is another impact of modernisation. Dancing in circle by a group is a typical style of most of the folk-dances, and this is also applicable to Bihunach of both Bihuwati and Bihuwa. Another style followed in Rati Bihu, Jeng Bihu and Hunchari is that one or a few members of the group dance in front, and other sing songs and play Bihubadya by positioning in a semi- circle. In the modern Bihutoli particularly in showcasing programmes several new choreographs have been included in Bihuwati's Bihunach. At present majority of the groups of Bihuwati follow these choreographs in addition to the said two traditional styles. The hard-core protectionists of the traditional form of Bihu-culture are of course criticising these new kinds of choreograph. On the other hand, those who are in favour of the new choreographs have the opinion that it is need of the situation - as Bihunach is now performed in modern stage as performing art, the new choreographs are essentials for decorous presentation.

Impacts of modernisation on Bihutoli

The impacts of modernisation on present day Bihutoli of the state need to be discussed from the following 3 dimensions:

a. Impacts on items of expenditure

b. Impacts on promotion of prototypical Bihunach, Bihunam and the traditional programmes.

c. Impacts on folk artists.

Impacts of modernisation on items of expenditure of Bihutoli

At present, the budgets of stage-based Bihutoli of the state ranged from Rs. 5 to Rs. 30 lakh. Many of these Bihutoli spend major portion of the budget mainly on 3 kinds of items: a) Honorarium to the invited celebrity artists who perform programmes on modern songs and modern Bihugeet with several western musical instruments. b) Construction and decoration of stage and Pandel. c) Arrangement of sophisticated sound technologies. Since mid of the decade of eighties, an upward trend has been witnessed regarding expenditure of the stage-based Bihutoli on these items. Only a few of the stage-based Bihutoli have been spending substantial amount of the budgets on programmes of Bihunach, traditional Bihu-programmes, and folk dance of ethnic groups.

On the contrary, the budgets of open-air Bihutoli ranged from 2 to 10 lakh. There is no expenditure on stage and on celebrity artists in such a Bihutoli. Major portion of the budget is spent on programmes on the traditional music-cum dance programmes of Bohag Bihu, and of ethnic groups. Moreover, such Bihutoli also spend some amount of the budget to arrange seminar, lecture, and discussion on selected topics on Bihu-culture by inviting distinguished scholars. Obviously these Bihutoli have been contributing sustainability towards preservation and promulgation of traditional form of Bihunach, Bihunam, Bihubadya and the traditional programmes of dance-cum-music of Bohag Bihu including Jeng Bihu, and Hunchari. However, the point to be pondered is that the numbers of this type of Bihutoli are much lesser than the other type – not more than 10 per cent of total Bihutoli organised throughout the state as part of celebrating Bohag Bihu.

Impacts of modernisation on essence of Bihutoli

In recent years, in some of the stage-based Bihutoli, Bihu-competitions are not organised. Programmes for showcasing of traditional music-cum dance programmes are also quite less in these Bihutoli. Instead, programmes of invited celebrity artists are organised with highest importance, and by spending major portion of the total budget. The sophisticated sound technologies of such Bihutoli are also mainly arranged and used for programmes of celebrity artists. Quite obviously, such a Bihutoli contributes negligibly towards Bihu-culture, and in a sense nullify the very essence for which a Bihutoli is to be ideally organised as part of celebrating Bohag Bihu.

As said earlier, Bihu-competitions are playing pivotal role in preserving, sustaining and promoting the prototypical Bihunach, Bihunam, Bihubadya, and the traditional dance-cum-music programmes of Bohag Bihu. Showcasing programmes of traditional music-cum dance events are also of course contributing to these purposes. Thus, Bihutoli ought to put adequate importance on arranging Bihu-competitions and showcasing programmes of prototypical Bihunach, Bihunam, Bihubadya, Hunchari and Jeng Bihu in order to promote the glorious intangible heritages of Bohag Bihu. But an opposite trend can clearly be observed in case of many of the stage-based Bihutoli of the state. More the magnitude and importance of such programmes in more number of Bihutoli higher the sustainability, spread, advancement and furtherance of the glorious heritages.

In recent years, sporadic occurrence of dispute relating to judgements Bihu-competitions in a few Bihutoli is appearing as a cause to foster aversion of organisers of some of the Bihutoli towards organising Bihu-competitions. In 2019, one of the groups of competitors used social media to express dissatisfaction regarding judgement of a Bihu-competition of high prize money, and they also made it news in Newspaper. Such episode would seriously affect the trend of Bihu-competitions and thereby affect the prototypical of Bihunach, Bihunach and the traditional dance-cum-music programmes of Bohag Bihu tremendously. It can well be advocated from several perspectives that all concerned need to take utmost care to check occurrence of such episode. Perhaps worth-mentioning that in the issue of 16-31 March, 2020 of the popular Assamese magazine 'Prantik', the author of this book has published an article on this subject-matter by explaining why such episode should be avoided to the maximum possible extent. [53]

Impact of Modernisation on Folk artists

Ideally, Bihutoli should be a boon for the folk artists especially Bihuwa and Bihuwati. But due to already discussed impacts of modernisations, the stage-based Bihutoli of the state by and large are failing to encourage them and in provisioning supports for them. The status and honorarium offered to folk artists in majority of the Bihutoli are several times lesser than that of the artists of modern songs. In fact, the Assamese folk-artists expecting Bihuwa and Bihuwati rarely get opportunity to perform programme in the Bihutoli organised in hundreds of places as part of celebrating Bohag Bihu. As a result, new generation of Assamese people is increasing becoming less interested towards the glorious and enormous intangible heritages of Assamese folk culture. They are rather inclined to establish themselves as artists of modern music, and thereby to tap the opportunity creating by most of the stage-based Bihutoli for such artists to establish as professionals. The folk artists of the state are thus seriously suffering from frustration. At this juncture, let me quote the following lines of acclaimed social scientist, Thomas A. Green: 'Folk music stressed its value as a representation of a special kind of community, one imagined to exist among a homogeneous group of non-elite people within a peasant, working- class ethnic or regional community'.[54]

Impact of Modernisation on Bihu-competitions

Collective celebration and participation are at the core of folk-dance and folk-music, and can be regarded as a basic characteristic. Rati Bihu, Jeng Bihu, and Hunchari are group programmes. Bihunach is therefore basically group dance as like most of the folk dance of the world. Even so, in modern era, a new kind of Bihu-competition namely, Bihuwati-competition has been introduced which is individualistic in spirit.

In Bihuwati-competition only one Bihuwati performs Bihunach along with singing Bihunam and playing Bihubadya. A group of Bihuwa play supportive role by playing Bihubadya and singing Bihunam. The prize is given to Bihuwati only. Interestingly, this very Bihuwati-competition gained more popularity. Till recently, many of the Bihutoli put prime importance on Bihuwati-competition, and in some of those only Bihuwati-competition was organised. This happened for more than three decades. Consequently, certain unwarranted impacts surfaced. In this context, intellectuals and social activists in the Bihu-culture started putting effort to develop awareness among all concerned to emphasis more on organising competitions of Hunchari and Jeng Bihu instead of Bihuwati-competition. Subsequently, in current years a downward trend of holding Bihuwati-competition and upward trend of organising Hunchari and Jeng Bihu has been observed. The author of this book published an article on this subject-matter by explaining why and how aspects in the 01-16 April, 2013 issue of Prantik.[55] Hem Borua expressed significance of collectiveness and nature in context to Bohag Bihu in the following lines: " The culture, arts and songs and dances of such a society are bound to be nature oriented. Assamese's Bahag Bihu is a people's festival of nature. People's art creations are not given to whims like the individual's creations of art. These art creations were social in inspiration. The main reason behind this fact is that ancient life was collective experience. To seek expression is man's natural instinct; self-expression is inherent in man. Without it art expression would have been impossible. Expression is the keystone of art."[56]

Impacts of Modernisation on rituals of Bihu festivals

As elucidated in chapter III, the Bihu festivals, particularly Bohag Bihu is outstandingly rich in rituals, and most of the rituals are of high value from several perspectives including personal wellbeing, spiritual wellness, and health-care, community cohesiveness, caring of cattle, and caring of implements of livelihood. Many of the Assamese families have been following the rituals to the possible extent in modern era too. Even so, there are vivid impacts of the changing socio-cultural, occupational and education situations of modern era in relation to rituals of the Bihu festivals. Such impacts are briefly stated below in 5 heads.

> ➤ Impacts on crop related rituals

> ➤ Impacts on rituals of offering reverence

> ➤ Impacts on health-care rituals

> ➤ Impacts on community feast of Magh Bihu

> ➤ Impacts on typical games of Bihu festivals

Impacts of modernisation on on crop related rituals

Due to occupational and educational changes in modern era, considerable Assamese families migrated to urban places, and left agricultural occupations. Moreover, agriculture has become secondary occupation in case of many of the families living in villages. Many families have given their agricultural land to tenants for cultivation. Further, replacement of bullocks by tractors and power-tillers has occurred substantially. Consequently, the ritual of 'caring bullock and cows' of Bohag Bihu has become quite obsolete for many of the families. Same point is applicable in case of the ritual of 'putting lamps in crop field' in Kati Bihu.

In present day circumstances too there is scope in many villages of the state to perform both the aforesaid rituals in festive mode with community participation. But it is not happening as expected. Majority of the families are performing both the rituals at family level. It can easily be perceived that this is happening mainly because of increasing self-centredness in the society. Noteworthy, that collective action is at the core of folk-culture. Most of elements of any folk culture including rituals, folklore and folk dance are subjected to collective actions. Without collective participation a component of folk culture loses its identity, essence and utilities to a great extent.

Impacts on rituals of offering reverence

In the modern era, in many of the affluent Assamese families, the young members are not keen to do Xewa to parents and other senior members of the family and community even at the occasions of the Bihu festivals. In other words, they tend to repulse the traditional manner of offering reverence to respected one particularly by doing Xewa in the traditional prostration pose. The most distinctive and first-rate ritual of doing Xewa to mother on the day of Manuh Bihu for obtaining blessings and breeze of Bichani is also widely neglected by many of the modern Assamese families.

Impacts on health-care rituals

Majority of Assamese families are following the health-care related rituals Bohag Bihu to the maximum practicable in present era too. These rituals are: a) Taking bath by applying the medicinal paste. b) Curry of 101 or 7 assorted herbs of medicinal value. C) Adorning of palm, toes and nails with Jetuka. However, a concern is that in recent years, a trend of replacing fresh Jetuka paste with the readymade Mehendy is growing. The fresh paste of Jetuka, and traditional way of its application is of more utility from health-care point of view. It is not less attractive too. Thus, replacement of Jetuka by Mehndi to adorn the parts of hands and feet in Bohag Bihu can be considered as superfluous adaptation of modernity.

Impacts on community feast of Magh Bihu

The community feast of Magh Bihu is in practice among Assamese families living in both rural and urban areas. Even so, concern is that a trend of celebrating the feast at family level or in smaller group is growing in current millennium. It is obviously due to increasing self-centredness as a consequence of modernity and abundance.

Impacts on typical games of Bihu festivals

Holding of Moh-yunj (buffalo-fight) in Magh Bihu has drastically reduced, and that of Bulbuli-fight has abolished completely due the said ordinance of the Supreme Court of India in the year 2014.

The Cowry-khel is rarely held at present day. It is happening mainly due to diversified occupations of the people and less availability of time for such a game which is played for several hours in night.

Koni-yunj (Egg fighting) is still in practice in some villages but with less vigour as well as participation than earlier. However, Koni-yunj is also organised in some of the Bihutoli.

Chapter XIV

PRESERVATION AND SAFEGUARDING OF INTANGIBLE RESOURCES OF BIHU FESTIVALS

Preservation and safeguarding of any traditional festival and its intangible constituents including rituals, music and dances has manifolds significances for a nation, race or community. Traditional festivals reflect inherited culture as whole - reflect heritage, legacy, values, beliefs, and wisdoms of people established through generations. Thus, these resources in a way define national, racial or communal identity and foster integrity. "Peoples' consciousness of their culture has a direct linkage with their diffusing identity".[57] Most of the constituents of traditional festivals of any race or community are immensely valuable. They are time tested, and generated and refined across many generations, and hence, can be regarded as gems of the culture.

In this context, the following lines are worth quoted from the forum theme summaries of the international event 'Preserving Culture and Heritage through Generations' held during May, 11-14, 2014 at Mimar Sinan University of Fine Arts, Turkey:

> Cultural heritage is the legacy of physical artefacts and intangible attributes of a group or society that are inherited from past generations, maintained in the present and bestowed for the benefit of future generations.

> Cultural heritage includes tangible culture such as buildings, monuments, landscapes, books, works of art, and artefacts. It also includes intangible culture traditions or living expressions inherited from our ancestors and passed on to our descendants, such as oral traditions, performing arts, social practices, rituals, festive events, knowledge and practices concerning nature and the universe or the knowledge and skills to produce traditional crafts intangible culture such as folklore, traditions, language, and knowledge, and natural heritage including culturally significant landscapes, and biodiversity. Whatever shape they take, these things form part

of a heritage, and this heritage requires active effort on our part in order to safeguard it. They may be significant due to their present or possible economic value, but also because they create a certain emotion within us, or because they make us feel as though we belong to something - a country, a tradition, a way of life.

> Cultural heritage affirms our identity as a people because it creates a comprehensive framework for the preservation of cultural heritage including cultural sites, old buildings, monuments, shrines, and landmarks that have cultural significance and historical value.

> The best way to preserve your cultural heritage, whatever it may be, is to share it with others.

> The importance of intangible cultural heritage is not the cultural manifestation itself but rather the wealth of knowledge and skills that is transmitted through it from one generation to the next.

> Cultural heritage and natural history of a nation has a very high value and is unique. It is an identity that can be introduced to the world.

The issues relating to preservation and safeguarding of the glorious intangible heritages of Bihu festivals have been discussed in previous chapters. This chapter presents a few selected efforts so far put in this direction by individuals, organisations and institutions.

Documentation of Bihunam in printed form

The need of documentation of folk music became vividly perceptible in some parts of the world as a result of the changed socio-cultural and economic scenario shaped by industrial revolution (1760- 1840). John Broadwood, a minister of Britain published a compilation of old

English songs in the year 1843, and that compilation is recognised as the first compilation of folk song in the world.

The first book on Bihu-culture, entitled as Bihu was published in 1914. It was written by Benudhar Rajkhowa. The first compilation of Bihunam is 'Akul Pathik' compiled by Dimbeswar Neog. It was published in 1922. The 2nd compilation of Bihunam namely, Bohagi was compiled by Nakul Chndra Bhunya and published in 1923. Another compilation of self-composed Bihunam of Mitradeva Mahanta was published in the year 1929.[58] A book of Bihunam in English language entitled as 'Bihu songs of Assam' authored by Prafulladutta Goswami was first put into print in 1934 , and later published in 1957. The book is a collection of 262 Bihu songs collected in 1921. Although the songs are in English, each song is later shown in original Assamese text.[59] A sizable compilation of Bihunam was documented by Dr. Lila Gogoi, and it was published in 1961. This very book 'Bihugeet and Bonghokha' has been serving as mostly read handbook of Bihunam since its publication till date. Several editions have so far been published. Then after, no considerable compilation of Bihunam was published till end of 20th century.

However, in the present millennium, several compilations have been published. A few of them are: Durlav Buragohain's Bihur Bhogjora (2005), and Dhonkoliya (2005). Ismail Hussain's Bihunamar Juruli (2009. Dr. Amarendra Gogoi's Bihunamar Borpera 1(2011), and Bihunamar Borpera-2(2012). Minakshi Lahon Das's Bihugeet aru Bihu (2012). A compilation of 1000 self-composed Bihunam of Mintumoni Saikia was published in 2014. Moreover, many Bihunam have also been documented in some of the books and articles on Bihu-culture. Worth mentioning that in majority of the compilations Bihunam are presented in classified format.

Documentation of Dholar-cheu and Bihunach in Printed form

As stated in the chapter on Bihubadhya, there are mainly 7 types of Dholar-cheu. Out of those, Budra-cheu and Hurali-cheu of Hunchari are most extensive, distinctive and superbly structured. Budra-cheu consists of total 13 definitely structured *bajna*. The Bihunach performed by Bihuwa in each of these 13 *bajna* is also definite and precisely structured with definite movements and poses. Hurali-cheu consists of total 6 precisely structured definite *bajna*, and the Bihunach performed by Bihuwa in each of these *bajna* is also definite and precisely structured. Moreover, selected Bihunam are also sung as integral part of Budra-cheu and Hurali-cheu, and the Bihunach performed by Bihuwa in these Bihunam are also typical. Thus Budra-cheu and Hurali-cheu are not only extensive but of very high standard intangible resource of Bohag Bihu.

However, both Budra-cheu and Hurali-cheu became obsolete in the format of Hunchari in which Xajowa-nachoni or Bihuwati perform Bihunach. The Dutia-cheu and its typical Bihunach also became obsolete in this format. Quite obviously, it appeared as a serious concern of the researchers and social activists of the field. In order to address this issue, in the early part of the decade of eighties of 20th century, the author of this book carried out an extensive research on all the Dholar-cheu of Hunchari and also the distinctively structured sets of Bihunach associated with the Dholar-cheu in order to document in written form. The documentations were published as a series of articles in a popular Newspaper 'Daink Janabhumi' in the year 1983. Later, the articles were compiled as book 'Rongali Bihur Nritya Geet' which was first published in 1987.

Documentation of intangible resources of Bihu festivals in audio and video formats

Assamese people have been substantially taping the opportunities of utilising electronic and information technologies for production, documentation and spread of Bihunam and Bihunach. Hundreds of audio cassettes, audio CD, video CD, and YouTube video of Bihunam and Bihunach have so far been produced. Bihunam were recorded in a Gramophone record for the first time by Bishnu Prasad Rabha in 1928. The name of the record was 'Bihuwati'. It was musical illustration based on Bihunam. Then in 1935, folk artist Bhola Saikia of Golaghat recoded Bihunam in Gramophone record. [60]

However, majority of the electronic and digital production on Bihunam and Bihunach produced so far are for commercial purpose. Only a few of them have been produced with exclusive purpose of preservation and spread of the original forms of Bihunach, Bihunam, rituals and the traditional programmes. A couple of efforts put exclusively with the purpose of promotion and preservation of the heritages of Bohag Bihu are briefly stated below.

The 'Bihu Surashya Sommitty, Assam.' produced a series of Video Compact Discs (VCDs) in mid part of the present decade which have later uploaded as YouTube videos. In these videos, the original forms of Rati Bihu, Jeng Bihu and Hunchari have been recorded in details and with enough prudence. These VCDs thus have become authentic resource to learn and practice the three traditional programmes as well as Bihunach, Bihunam and Bihubadya by maintaining the prototypical features. The 'Bihu Surashya Sommitty, Assam' also made free distribution of the VCDs to many of the schools of the state so that the students as well as new generation can learn and practice and Bihunach, Bihunam and Bihubadya, and the traditional programmes appropriately.

Moreover, a few researchers and social activists also produced VCDs as well as YouTube videos at individual level with the main purpose of preservation and spread of the prototypical forms of Bihunach, Bihunam Bihubadya, and the traditional programmes of those. Selected rituals of Bohag Bihu are also recorded in such VCDs. In this context, contributions of Bimala Gogoi Gohain are commendable. In 2005, she schemed and directed a VCD film entitled as 'Bohagi' and acted in a major role. Several rituals of Bihu festivals in addition to original forms of Rati Bihu and Jeng Bihu have been recorded in the film. Moreover, she has uploaded a series of short YouTube videos entitled as 'Project Otenga-Namor Hanchati' during 2018-19. The videos present several typical Bihunam and selected rituals of Bihu festivals with minor details. During mid-part of eighties of 20th century, the author of this book directed 3 audio cassettes in which several original Bihunam were recorded in original form. The names of the cassettes were Bopoti Xaahon, Bihutoli and Zangfai.

Another creditable contribution towards documentation of rituals has been made by an agricultural scientist, Dr. Sadiqul Hussain. In 2018 he uploaded a series of YouTube video on the plant species used in Bohag Bihu for preparation of the medicinal curry of 101 herbs. The video series entitled as '101 herbs and trees of Assam' present Assamese names, scientific names and parts to be used for the curry of all the 101 plant species along with photographs.

Training and Education on Bihu-culture

Bihu-workshops have been organising throughout the state for several decades with the objective of providing practical training on original forms of Bihunach, Bihunam, Bihubadya and traditional programmes of those. Such workshops are generally organised prior to commencement of Bohag Bihu for 3 to 15 days. They are mostly being organised at the initiatives of cultural bodies in various locations of the state. 'Bihu Surashya Sommitty, Assam' also organises Bihu-workshops in various places in the state.

Most recently, in 2020 the 'Assam Higher Secondary Education Council' introduced a course on 'Bihu' at higher secondary level. The course curriculum include lessons on various aspects of the Bihu festivals and their cultural heritages including Bihunach, Bihunam, and Bihubadya, Hunchari, Rati Bihu, Jeng Bihu, and also origin and evolution of the Bihu festivals. The course includes both theory and practical.

Contributions of 'Bihu Surashya Sommitty, Assam'

'Bihu Surashya Sommitty, Assam' was established in the year 2010 with the purpose of safeguarding, preserving, educating and spreading of the intangible heritages of the Bihu festivals. It is a non-governmental organisation registered under Society act. At present, it is the most extensive organisation of this kind with district level committees in most of the districts of Brahmaputra valley of Assam. This year i.e in 2020, the organisation initiated establishment of 'Centres for Study and Research on Traditional culture' across the state with the purpose of promoting regular study, research and training on various intangible cultural resources of Assam and North-eastern India. More than 150 centres in different localities of the state have been established till end of the month of October 2020.

One of the commendable programmes of Bihu Surashya Sommitty, Assam was production and distribution of the series of VCDs mentioned earlier. Another remarkable effort carried out by the organisation is preparation and production of the set of all-inclusive guidelines of Bihu -competitions in the year 2011. As mentioned earlier, at present, majority of the Bihutoli of the state and all concerned follow this set of guidelines. The other kinds of efforts the Bihu Surashya Sommitty, Assam has been putting for the purposes are as follow:

> Organising seminars on issues and thrust areas relating to safeguarding, preservation, practice and spread of archetypical Bihu -culture.

> Preparation and production of books and periodicals on Bihu -culture

> Organising Bihu-workshops, and also training programmes of Master Trainers of Bihunach, Bihubadya, Hunchari and Jeng Bihu.

> Felicitating distinguished artists, researchers and authors for commendable works on traditional culture and heritages of Assam.

Contributions of Media towards Bihu-culture

Various media including Newspapers, Magazines, Souvenirs, Radio, TV channels and other social media like YouTube and Facebook have been playing impressive roles in promoting, safeguarding, preserving, and spreading of archetypical intangible resources of the Bihu festivals as well as traditional Assamese culture.

All the Assamese Newspapers and majority of the Assamese magazines have been publishing special issues on the occasion of Bohag Bihu. Moreover, articles on various subject-matters of the Bihu festivals are also published in normal issues of Assamese Newspapers at the time of all the three Bihu festivals. Furthermore, many of the Bihutoli publish souvenirs with the main purpose of publishing articles on Bohag Bihu and Assamese culture as a whole. Thus, substantial numbers of articles on the various topics of Bihu festivals are published every year, and majority of those are primarily meant for promoting, safeguarding, preserving, and spreading of archetypical intangible resources of the Bihu festivals. Furthermore, Newspapers are serving as guard by publishing News, News-stories and interviews timely to address issues with the purpose of safeguarding the prototypical intangible heritages of Bihu festivals.

Radio has been promoting the cause for several decades by broadcasting programmes on archetypical Bihunam, musical drama, articles and discussion programmes.

TV channels have been contributing in several ways. All the Assamese TV channels are prompt enough to address issues for safeguarding the traditional Bihu-culture by broadcasting News and Talk-shows. TV channels are also substantially broadcasting the intangible heritages of Bihu festivals through in-situ coverage and recording, and also by broadcasting news stories on traditional artists. Furthermore, couple of channels have been broadcasting Bihu-competitions.

In recent years, social media such as Facebook, WhatsApp, and YouTube are also playing significant role for the purpose. Assamese people are quite active in using social media to share information, ideas and other inputs relating to Bihu festivals and their intangible resources. They are also proactive to safeguard those.

Chapter XV

POSTULATIONS ON ORIGIN OF BIHU FESTIVALS

There is difference of opinions regarding the question – which ethic group originally initiated celebration of Bihu festivals. There is also difference of opinions among researchers regarding the origin of the word 'Bihu '. Of course, according to majority of the researchers and authors, the origin of the Bihu festivals is of Austroasiatic culture, and thus, Bihu festivals are of more than 5000 years old. This very postulation is supported by following fact based analysis:

1. Austroasiatic people are mainly agrarian, and they are remarkably fun loving. They celebrate various religious and agricultural festivals. Dancing and singing in addition to religious rituals are integral part of most of their folk festivals.

2. A study carried out recently by author of this book reveals that all the races and ethnic groups of Austroasiatic people throughout Asia have been celebrating agrarian folk festivals similar to Bihu festivals - since many centuries till date. There are 7 large Austroasiatic races in the present day world: Kinh or Vietnamese of Vietnam, Khmer or Cambodians of Cambodia, Filipino of Philippines, Marina of Madagascar, Mon of Mon state of Myanmar, and Khasia and Jayantia of Meghalaya state. Each of these races has been celebrating more than one agrarian folk festival similar to Bihu festivals. The study also reveals that all the smaller Austroasiatic ethnic groups living in various parts of India and Bangladesh have also been celebrating agrarian folk festivals. They include Santal, Munda, Prajapati, Juwanhu, Hu and Orang. Moreover, some tribes of Kinh, Khmer, Filipino and Mon in various parts of Asia have also been celebrating agrarian folk festivals like Bihu festivals by maintaining distinctive rituals and activities of own ethnic culture. (The study yet to be published elsewhere).

3. Most of the agrarian festivals celebrating by various Austroasiatic races and ethnic groups throughout Asia are related to cultivation of paddy crop.

4. In the aforesaid study, a total of 157 numbers of on-going agrarian folk festivals in Asia have been explored. These 157 numbers of agricultural folk festivals have been celebrating by 98 numbers of ethnic-groups including the above mentioned seven big races. Out of these 98 ethnic-groups including the big races, 19 (19.38%) are Austroasiatic, and they have been celebrating total 37 (23.56 %) of the on-going agrarian folk festivals similar to Bihu festivals. Worth mentioning that in the study attempt has been made to explore all the on-going agrarian folk festivals in Asia. However, total numbers of ethnic-groups celebrating agrarian folk festivals and also total number of on-going agrarian folk festivals in Asia might be more than that explored in the study. In other words, it cannot be claimed that the study explored all the on-going agrarian folk festivals in Asia.

5. Out of the 37 numbers of agrarian folk festivals celebrating by 19 Austroasiatic ethnic groups as well as races, 11 are celebrated prior to land preparation of Paddy crop with the basic purpose of praying all round growth of the crop so as to obtain bumper harvest. Two of the festivals are celebrated at growth stage of Paddy crop with the basic purpose of protecting the crop from pests and other evils. The rest 22 are celebrated as harvesting festivals of Paddy crop with the basic purpose of thanksgiving God(s) for the harvest and start enjoying the harvest. In other words, out of 37 numbers of agrarian folk festivals celebrating by 19 Austroasiatic ethnic groups, 11 are similar to Bohag Bihu, 2 are similar to Kati Bihu and rest 22 are similar to Magh Bihu on the basis on purposes as well as stages of cultivation of Paddy crop.

6. Several rituals of the agrarian folk festivals celebrating by the Austroasiatic ethnic groups as well as races found to be analogous to those of the three Bihu festivals.

7. The basic purposes and majority of the traditional rituals of agrarian folk festivals of Asia reflect beliefs of Animism religion. This is applicable to basic purposes and some of the rituals of the three Bihu festivals.

8. Most of the ethnic groups of Asia including the Austroasiatic celebrate the main agrarian folk festival for more than one day. In case of many of the festivals different days of the festivals are called in different names, and definite rituals are performed in each day. Thus, it is analogous to our Xaat Bihu of Bohag Bihu. As stated earlier, Xaat Bihu encompasses 7 days with specific name of each day, and definite rituals are performed in each day.

9. Several items, activities as well as rituals relating to the Bihu festivals can be considered as of Austroasiatic culture. [61,62,63,64]

All the above points indicate that Austroasiatic who were the earliest inhabitants of Assam, and lived in this part of land for more than two thousand years celebrated the three Bihu festivals. In other words, Austroasiatic are the original initiator of Bihu festivals. Hem Barua elucidated this topic quite explicitly: "The most ancient inhabitants of Assam are of Ausro-Asiatic family; Austro-Asiatics were agriculturists. They raised potatoes, paddy, pulses and betel-nuts and leaves. ... Around these agricultural activities grew different festivities i.e different items of culture. In course of time, naturally enough, there were exchanges of these cultural types with other indigenous cultural types of the time. For instance, in our language there are still in use of words like *nangal* which means 'ploughshare' in the Austroloid language. The Austro-Asiatics are a dreamy sort of people, indolent in habit and temperament. From the point of temperament, they were attuned to aesthetic creation. Even today in places where the Austro-

Asiatics lived there are evidences of festivals devoted to the seasons. In the areas of Java, Nicobar and Australia wherever there are evidences of Austroloid culture, there are evidences of ancient cultural types also. …. Although the Austroloid cultural pattern was submerged to a certain extent in the plains-areas of Assam by Mongoloid, Bodo, Dravidian and Aryan cultural trends, the Austroloid pattern did not completely die out. Glimmerings of this still exit as substratum. The habit of chewing betel-nut and betel-leaves of the Assamese is a relic of Austroloid culture. The Bihu that originally emerged in this peasant society was ultimately absorbed and assimilated by the Aryans. Although the Aryan cultural pattern thus super-imposed itself, the Austroloid cultural pattern continued to exert its influence. This is the significance of the Bihu." [65]

Chapter XVI

POSTULATION ON ORIGIN OF HUNCHARI

There is no solid documented factual information about when Assamese people started Hunchari as a programme of Bohag Bihu. However, based on historical indicative evidences, some researchers postulate that the event was initiated by Tai-Ahom people. The Tai-Ahom ethnic group entered into the land of Assam in 1228 under the leadership of Chaolung Siu-ka-Pha, a Tai prince with 9000 followers. As per historians they came from either Mong Mao of south china or Hukawn valley in Myanmar. The group established Ahom kingdom in almost entire Brahmaputra valley and ruled for about 600 years (1228 -1826 AD). Tai-Ahom people started the programme of Hunchari based on one of their original music-cum-dance event called as Ru-cheng-ri, and in due course of time most of the other ethnic groups of the state also organised the programme in their villages. In Ru-cheng-ri the Tai people perform dance and music by moving on roads in group, and families at their gates offer items like tamul-pan, rice and eggs. The word Hunchari has evolved from off the cuff from the word Ru-cheng-ri".[66] Various Tibeto-Burman ethnic groups living in Assam before Tai-Ahom came. These groups continued living even after Tai-Ahom established kingdom. Socio-cultural intermixing of Tai-Ahom with various ethnic groups of Tibeto-Burman took place extensively. Hunchari was adopted by majority of the Tibeto-Burman ethnic groups. However, in due course of time Hunchari has been adopted by most of the ethnic groups of Assam, and also influenced the same.

According to historians, Hunchari was remarkably promoted first by Ahom king Pramatta Singha who reigned during 1744 to 1751 AD. The king built a gorgeous double storied pavilion for beholding cultural programmes and games. This stunning pavilion is considered as the oldest amphitheatre in Asia. The king put great importance on Hunchari, and at the occasion of Bohag Bihu invited Hunchari-dals of villages to perform Hunchari at Rang-Ghar. This tradition was also followed by other Ahom kings who ruled after him.

Chapter XVII

POSTULATIONS ON ORIGIN OF THE WORD BIHU

Although it can well be postulated that Bihu festivals might have initiated by Austroasiatic people when they lived in Assam during 3000 BC to 1000 BC, but there is dearth of evidential facts to postulate that word Bihu is originated from Austroasiatic language. It is quite obvious that Austroasiatic people named the three Bihu festivals in their Austroasiatic language. But a word in Austroasiatic languages sound-alikes Bihu and reveals meaning of festival could not be traced. Hence, most of the researchers opined that the word Bihu might have come from a language of certain aboriginal ethnic group other than Austroasiatic. Of-course, there is difference of opinions of researchers regarding specific ethnic group from which the word 'Bihu' is originated.

Several Tibeto-Burman ethnic groups of people living in Assam have been celebrating agrarian folk festivals similar to Bihu festivals with own ethnic distinctiveness and in names of own ethnic languages. The names of these festivals are similar to the word Bihu. Based on this observation, the author of this book expressed in his book entitled as 'Bihu Binandia' that the word Bihu might have come to Assamese language from the language or dialect of any of the ethnic groups who have been celebrating agrarian folk festival similar to Bihu festivals in a name sound-alike the word Bihu.[67] The author elucidated as follows: The Deuri people called Bohag Bihu as Bisu; Bi-means very much and Su means joyfulness. The Bodo people called such festival as Boikhu, and their festival similar to Bohag Bihu as Boishagu. The Dimasa people called such a festival as Busu which means enjoying together by singing and dancing. Moreover, the Tiwa people called such a festival as Pihu while their festival similar to Bohag Bihu is called as Baisag pihu. Rabha people celebrate a festival similar to Bohag Bihu called as Baikhu. The basic purposes, activities and rituals of these festivals of different tribes are similar to that of

Bihu festivals. Moreover, these festivals are celebrated corresponding to the same stages of cultivation of *Sali-* paddy.

All the five ethnic groups mentioned above are of Kachari ethnic group of Tibeto-Burman. Hence, it can be postulated that the word Bihu is originated from any of the ethnic groups of Kachari people of Assam. Worth mentioning that according to a couple of researchers the assimilation of Austroasiatic people took place relatively more intensively with Kachari people. Bishnu Prasad Rabha, the Assamese legend in the fields of culture and literature opined that the word Bihu comes from Bodo language. Dinesh Gogoi and few others also opined that the word Bihu might have originated from any of the ethnic language of Tibeto-Burman groups.

A few authors opined that the word Bihu is originated from Tai language of Tai-Ahom people who are living in Assam since 1228 AD, and celebrating the three Bihu festivals extensively. According to Dr. Lila Gogoi, Bouthan Thon Gogoi and few others, the word Bihu evolved from the Tai word Boihu.[68,69] Joykanta Gandhia and few others expressed that the word Bihu might have evolved from the Tai words Pi-hu-u or Poihu.[70] As expressed by Dr. Lalit Syam Pi means year, hu means beginning, and u means fun and joy.[71] Dr. Nagen Saikia also expressed that the word Bihu might have evolved from Tai language.[72]

A few authors including Dr. Nabin Chandra Sarma, Dr. P.C. Goswami, Trolukya Bhattacharyya postulated that the word Bihu may be evolved from Sanskrit word Bishuva or Bishuvan which denotes Mahabishuba Sankranti. [73,74,75]

Chapter XVIII

AGRARIAN FESTIVALS OF ETHNIC GROUPS OF ASSAM SIMILAR TO BIHU FESTIVALS

As stated earlier a few ethnic groups of Assam have been celebrating agrarian folk festivals similar to Bihu festivals by maintaining distinctiveness of own ethnic cultures. The basic purposes of celebrating these festivals and overall nature of the celebration are same as of Bihu festivals. The seasons of celebration are the same, and are associated with Paddy cultivation or paddy-based Jhum cultivation. Worshiping the God or deities as per beliefs of an ethnic group is integral part of such a festival. Although some of the activities and rituals are same with the Bihu festivals but some are different. The ethnic groups called these festivals in specific names in their own languages or dialects. Moreover, such an ethnic group does not celebrate the festivals exactly in the same days of Bihu festivals. This chapter present such agrarian folk festivals of a few ethnic groups of Assam.

Agrarian folk festivals of Rabha people

The main agrarian folk festival of Rabha people is called as Baikhu. It is celebrated before starting Paddy cultivation in which they worship a deity called as Baihku for rain. The main purpose of celebrating the festival is to obtain healthy growth of the crop leading to bumper harvest. The associated purpose is to gain all round welfare of families and society. Several rituals are similar to that of Bohag Bihu including the ritual of caring of bullocks and cows. Traditionally the festival is celebrated for seven days. Each day has definite name, and each day definite rituals are performed. During the festival they worship several God and Goddesses namely Surari, Nakati, Tamai, Daduri, Kancha, and Bisahari in addition to Baikhu. They sing two kinds of traditional songs ritualistically during the festival. They are Haimaru and Mare-gan. A distinctive ritual of Baikhu festival is Nak-junkey in which a group appointed by village head sprinkles rice-flour on rooftops of houses of the villages by singing Mare-gan. These very songs are meant for worshiping the snake goddess Bisahari. On the first day of the festival, they also perform the ritual of bathing and caring of cows and bullocks by following own ritualistic actions.

The Rabha people also celebrate two other agrarian folk festivals namely, Longa-mara and Hamjar. The Longa-mara festival is celebrated at growth stage of Paddy crop with purpose of worshiping specific goddess so as to protect crops, cattle and human being from all enemies and evils. In Hamjar festival they catch fishes as community in common water source such as *beel* and river. They perform a traditional dance called as Naksung-reni in this festival. In this festival, some of the sections of Rabha people prepare a traditional cuisine of medicinal value called Dinga-sak. It is prepared from broken rice and leaves of Vedai lota plant (Paederia foetida L.) by cooking in bamboo internode.

Agrarian folk festivals of Mising people

Mising people celebrate mainly three distinctive agrarian folk festivals namely, Ali-Aye-Ligang, Po:rag and Amrok.

Ali-Aye-Ligang festival is celebrated in the month of Fagun of Assamese calendar for five days at the occasion of sowing seeds in Ahu-paddy cultivation. Ceremonial sowing of seeds takes place in paddy field on the first day, and a couple of deities are worshiped for good crop growth and protection of crop leading to bumper harvest. In Mising language, the word Ali means seed or root, Aye means growth, and Ligang means sowing or planting. In this festival, group of boys and girls in each village perform traditional dance programmes at courtyard of every household. The programme is similar to Hunchari of Bohag Bihu. The traditional dance performed in this festival is called as Gumraag dance, and songs are called Oi-nitom.

Po:rag festival is celebrated after harvest of *Ahu*-paddy for five days. Two deities, Chedi-melo and Doyli-polo are worshiped in this festival by expressing thanks for harvest and praying for all round welfare. Community feast and various traditional dances and singing programmes are integral part of the festival. It is also called as Nara-singa-Bihu. The festival ends with a prayer dance called as Ponu-nunam.

In Amrok festival, Mising people offer food prepared from harvested crop to ancestors and respected persons of the society. Community feast is organised and Pakso-monan dance and Oi-nitam songs are performed.

In addition to the said three distinctive festivals, at present, many of the Mising families also celebrate three Bihu festivals.

Agrarian folk festivals of Bodo people

Bodo people celebrate Boisakhu festival before starting cultivation of Sali paddy, and Mogu domsiang festival after harvesting the crop. The basic purposes, dates of celebration, and some of the rituals of these two festivals are same with Bohag Bihu and Magh Bihu. However, there is difference regarding religious rituals associated with the festivals. They worship definite deities in the festivals. The deity primarily worshiped in Boisakhu festival is called as Bathou. The traditional dance associated with Boisakhu festival is called as Bagurumba dance. Bodo people called Kati Bihu as Kati Gasa light lamps at the foot of the Siju tree (Euphorbia neriifolia). They also celebrate a festival at the occasion first consumption of harvest. It is called as Bagkham-Grolbi-Jonai.

Agrarian folk festivals of Dimasa people

Demasa people celebrate mainly three agrarian folk festivals related to Jhum cultivation. They celebrate Hajagerowa festival at the occasion of sowing seeds in Jhum plot, Maisyagerowa festival at the occasion of weeding, and Bushu-dima after harvesting of the crops of Jhum cultivation. Religious rituals are performed in each of the festivals with great importance, and definite deities are worshiped following specific ritualistic activities. Two kinds of traditional dances namely Kram–jung-mai-duba, and Bai-ma-jai are performed in Bushu-dima festival. The Kram–jung-mai-duba dance is performed by both males and females by reflecting various activities of Jhum cultivation. In Bai-ma-jai dance females perform typical dance by taking traditional dishes in hands. Dimasa people also celebrate Gathi Sainjora at the time of Kati Bihu with same purpose.

Agrarian folk festivals of Karbi people

The main agricultural folk festival of Karbi people is Dehel–kasirdomo-ba. It is celebrated for three days before starting Paddy cultivation, and several deities are worshiped for good crop growth and bumper harvest. The traditional dance, Murik-pansi is performed in this festival. Another agrarian folk festival, Mono-ke-an is celebrated by Karbi people at the interval of five years. The main purpose is to worship the deity called as Clan-makar so as to obtain blessings for good harvest in paddy cultivation and all round welfare of people and society. Some of the Karbi tribes also celebrate two harvesting festivals–Rongker and Domahi. In both the festivals they worship and offer thankfulness to various deities for the harvest. The deity worshiped in Domahi festival is called as Hemaphuk - the deity of crops.

Agrarian folk festivals of Garo people

The Garo people of Assam celebrate mainly 5 festivals relating to Jhum cultivation. They celebrate Grandik ba festival at the occasion of cleaning forest for Jhum cultivation. They celebrate Jama Siang at the initiation of seed sowing in Jhum cultivation, and the Mezek Sima festival at growth stage of crops. At the occasion of harvesting crops of Jhum cultivation the Garo people celebrate Medong Rauna festival, and after harvesting of crops Wangala festival. Various sections of Garo people also celebrate some additional agrarian folk festivals.

Agrarian folk festivals of Deuri people

Deuri people celebrate Ibanku Bisu festival before starting Sali-paddy cultivation, and after harvesting of the crop they celebrate Magiya Bisu. Many of the activities and dance programmes of the festivals are similar to Bohag Bihu and Magh Bihu but of own ethnic distinctiveness. Ibanku Bisu is celebrated for seven days, and one of its important rituals is 'caring bullocks and cows'. In this festival, Deuri people also perform Hunchari similar to that of Bohag Bihu. The main ritualistic activities of Magiya bisu are similar to that of Magh Bihu which includes Mezi, community feast and traditional games. Of course, Deuri people follow own ethnic rituals in both the festivals as per their religious beliefs.

Agrarian folk festivals of Hajong, Tiwa and Koch-Rajbonshi, Moran

The agrarian folk festivals of these four ethnic groups are mostly same with the Bihu festivals. However, Hajong, Tiwa and Koch-Rajbonshi called the festivals in own ethnic names. On the other hand, the Moran people celebrate Bohag Bihu with a couple of distinctive norms and rituals. As because ethnic distinctiveness are not extensive so grouped under one heading.

Hajong people celebrate two harvesting festivals namely, Biswa and Pusna. Biswa is celebrated before starting Sali-paddy cultivation, and Pusna is celebrated after harvest of Sali-paddy. The time of celebration, basic purpose and most of the rituals of Biswa and Pusna festivals are the same as of Bohag Bihu and Magh Bihu respectively. Hajong people also celebrate three more agrarian festivals mostly at family level: Paila roa- the first paddy transplantation ceremony. Ag-ona – the ceremony of bringing home the first harvest of paddy from field. Kanchi-dowa - the ceremony for completion of harvesting of paddy.

The Koch-Rajbonshi people celebrate the festivals 'Bishuwa' at the time of Bohag Bihu for seven days, and follow rituals similar to Bohag Bihu.

Tiwa people celebrate three festivals related to Sali-paddy cultivation. The purposes, rituals, dances are same with the three Bihu festivals. The difference mainly exists in naming. They called the three festivals as Boisag Pishu, Kartika-Pishu and Maghiya Pishu.

The Moran people living in Upper-Assam celebrate Bohag Bihu with certain distinctive norms and rituals. The dance events Rati Bihu and Dharma-Hunchari of this ethnic group are distinctive.

Chapter XIX

AGRARIAN FESTIVALS SIMILAR TO BIHU FESTIVALS IN ASIA

Various races and ethnic groups in different parts of Asia have been celebrating quite a large numbers of agrarian folk festivals. Being agrarian folk festivals the purposes of these festivals are basically related to crops cultivation –worshiping the God(s) for good harvest. Moreover, the rituals, games, dance and music of these festivals are by and large similar in nature.

A study was carried out to know about the agrarian folk festivals celebrating by different races and ethnic groups in various parts of Asia continent. A total of 162 agrarian folk festivals celebrating in Asia have been studied. Out of these 162 agrarian folk festivals briefs about 15 festivals are presented in this chapter. These festivals are selected by taking into consideration of interesting similarities with Bihu festivals with regard to purpose, rituals, games, dance and music.

Amis Harvest festival of Taiwan

Amis Harvest Festival is an age old agrarian festival of the aboriginal indigenous tribes of Taiwan broadly called as Amis tribes. They live mainly in Taitung and Hualien areas of the country. Normally, different tribes select different times to celebrate the festival during July, August, and September. The features of celebration among the tribes are similar but not exactly the same. Some tribes celebrate it for 3 days and some other for 7 days. Some of the tribes celebrate it twice - after harvesting of Millets and Paddy.

Basically, the main purpose of the festival is thanksgiving the ancestral Gods for successful harvest of crop, and worshiping for bumper harvest in coming years, and also for all-round welfare of the society. In addition to the religious rituals, community dinner, dancing, camp-fire party and traditional games are integral part of the colourful festival. The rituals and all festivities are carried out by abiding definite norms and with systematic preparations. Currently, besides the traditional celebration, the festival has become an attraction of large numbers of tourists. Salient aspects of this wonderful festival are as hereunder:

Before the night of first day of the festival, a big community dinner called as Malafi Ko Niar is organised in which all the members across age and gender participate. Participating in the dinner is regarded as the way to unite the members of the tribe, and a great opportunity for all the members of the tribe to strengthen their relationships. According to the traditional custom, guests from other villages as well as tribes are invited to the dinner. As a pre-festival activity, selected young men go to the selected villages to invite important guests.

Every year, well before the festival, the leaders of the tribe meet to decide on various aspect of celebrating the festival – to decide the day of ceremony – to fix fee to be collected from each family for the dinner party – to constitute various committees to carry out different works- to selecting special guests to be invited. According to the traditional custom, the beef should be the main dish for the big community feast Malafi Ko Niar, and the number of cows butchered is also decided in this meeting.

The ceremony on the first day of the festival is hosted by the priest of the tribe, who is in charge of the sacrificial ritual. He is regarded as a knowledgeable and wise man. Since all the ceremonies of the Amis are closely related to the farming, as a part of ritual the priest provides important information and instructions relating the farming activities such as ploughing, sowing, weeding, and harvesting and so on. It is necessary for a priest to possess enough knowledge on the various aspect relating to tribe including calendar, weather, history of the tribe, dancing programmes and how to communicate with the God(s).

At the night of the last day of the festival, an especial traditional singing and dancing programme is held which is at present informally called as the **Night of Valentine's Day**. The young Amis men and women take part in this singing and dancing programme to choose their partners. The programme starts with dancing of men, and after sometimes girls join in dancing. The girls and boys dance around the campfire under the moonlight and singing and dancing last to the next morning. In this programme each young men keeps a bag on his back. If a girl finds a boy she likes, she actively stands by the boy and dance with him. If she likes to propose the boy as life partner, she puts a beetle-nut in the boy's bag. If the boy accepts the proposal then he hand overs the bag to the girl, and thus, their agreement on marriage is confirmed. The programme is organised by abiding definite traditional norms strictly.

Adult ceremony is another important programme of Amis Harvest festival. It is organised at interval of 3 to 8 years based of tradition of different tribes. The main purpose of this ceremony is to bestow recognition to suitable young men of the tribe as adult. In Amis tribes, the age structure of males is always at the centre of all spheres of life and society. The age structure of males plays key roles in deciding the tribe's social rules, moral education, learning ability and the capability to protect the tribe from the invasion of other tribes.

In the adult ceremony, the prospective young men i.e the candidates have to go through certain kinds of tests in order to get the recognition as adults. Race of running is the most common test. Amis tribe's age structure is divided into three groups: the elder, the adult and the adolescents. The age bracket of the candidates is from thirteen to twenty. Before participating in adult ceremony as a candidate, a young man has to undergo definite training programme. During the training, the young men learn various important subject-matters including life skills and obedience. On the last day of adult ceremony, the candidates host a dinner party in honour of the elders. Each candidate contributes a barrel of wine and a chick for the feast.

The elders and the priest tell good words to them and wish them good luck.

An American journalist Tony Coolidge published an interesting article on present day status of celebration of festival in 2016. The interesting features reported in the article entitled as 'Amis Harvest festival -Colourful Celebration of Life's Abundance' are as follows: "Forty communities are hosting the Amis Harvest Festival every year. Traveling from Hualien, in the middle of Taiwan's East Coast, down to Taitung, in Taiwan's Southeast corner, one can find Amis Harvest Festivals scheduled in conjunction with when millet is harvested in their area. The celebrations, which can last from three to seven days, typically begin in the middle of July and conclude at the end of August. According to the Council of Indigenous Peoples, the largest aboriginal tribe in Taiwan is the Amis tribe, with over 190,000 members. Visitors can experience authentic Indigenous culture in Taiwan, participating in ceremonies that have been performed for hundreds of years. Outsiders can become emotional as they hold hands with villagers, share millet wine, and experience the rituals, learning about their meanings".[76]

Pah Re Re festival of Thailand

Pah Re Re is an age-old agrarian festival of Nyah Kur tribe of Chaiyaphum province in the north east of Thailand. This hilly tribe celebrates this festival prior to seed sowing in rice cultivation. The time coincides with the Thai Songkram or New Year festival of Thailand. The Thai Songkram starts on the day of Sangkran as per Luner calendar which normally befalls on 13th April.

Nyah Kur people celebrate the Pah Re Re festival for several days, and perform programme of singing and dancing in nights in which both females and males participate. Similarities with Rati Bihu and Bihunam can be perceived in the nature of the programme and also regarding subject-matters and style of singing the songs. The technique of vibrato is used to decorate beautiful melody. Almost same melody is repeatedly maintained throughout the songs. The themes of the songs are about love, courtship, flirtation, concerns, care, family's wellbeing, livelihood and unity of the community. Moreover, enquiring and answering questions by means of songs take place between females and males – similar with Joranam of Rati Bihu. The dance and songs of the festival are called Pah Re Re.

The Nyah Kur is the ethnic group native to Thailand known as Chao Bon in Thai. They are closely related to Mon Khmer. The Nyah Kur language is a sister language to the Mon language of Burma the two of which constitute the only languages of the Monic branch of Austroasiatic language family.

Otaue Shinji festival of Japan

Otaue shinji or Rice-planting festival is one of the most famous festivals in the Kansai region of Japan. The festival is held on June 14 every year at the famous Sumiyoshi Taisha Shrine and is an ancient Shinto festival to pray for obtaining bumper harvest in rice cultivation. The festival is said to have taken place every year since 211 AD. The Japanese word Otaue refers to the process of rice transplanting. Similar Rice-planting festivals can be found all over Japan among different communities as well as tribes in various names. Otaue shinji is the most famous, unique, colourful and magnificent among those.

The festival starts off with ploughing of rice field by wooden ploughs pulled by decorated oxen and men. All the participants dressed in brightly coloured traditional outfits. After ploughing a special purification ritual of rice seedlings take place. Several deities are worshiped in this ritual. Then the priests present the purified rice seedlings to be planted. Then the female participants plant the purified rice seedlings in the paddy field. Spectacular dance performances and songs go along with planting of seedlings. The menfolk participate by singing traditional songs and playing musical instruments. The dance is called as Sumiyoshi Dance. Traditional Japanese musical instruments such as Shamisen and Taiko drums are accompanied with the songs and dance.

The Japanese believe that dancing and music enhances the vitality of the rice grains. They also believe that powerful spirits dwell inside the rice seedlings and the dancing entertains the spirits so they grow healthy leading to bumper harvest. This belief is reflected in the songs and dance.

Do Son Buffalo Fighting festival of Vietnam

This traditional Buffalo Fighting festival is held in Do Son Town of Vietnam annually on the ninth day of the eighth month of the lunar calendar. The festival is associated with Water God worshipping ceremony of the Hien Sinh custom for prosperity and happiness. Moreover, it is believed that Buffalo and Buffalo-fight typically express the martial spirit. It has been celebrating since the 18th century. The event is organised flamboyantly and systematically by following definite steps, rituals and norms.

On the day of the festival, a worshiping ceremony is held in every village to pray for the victory at the buffalo fight. This worshiping ceremony lasts until lunch time. Then after the Buffalo Fighting event takes place at Do Son town majestically with great splendours and participation of large number of people. People including organisers, competitors, and spectators wear colourful traditional attires.

The festival at Do Son town takes off with a colourful procession. The most attractive and significant component of the procession is that a big procession-chair is carried by six strong young men in royal dress and by following definite norms.

The arena of the fight is arranged colourfully. Each of the participating buffalo is decorously adorned by covering part of the body with shining red cloth and by binding red band around the horns. Each buffalo is brought to the arena by a small group majestically who wear definite colourful dress. The buffalos are then taken to near the fighting ring by 24 young men. Then after a dance programme is held. The young men dance and wave flags as the two teams of troops take their positions in the fighting ground. The dance was mingled with the ebullient sound of drums and gongs, bringing a hectic atmosphere to the festival.

After the dance, the fights of buffaloes start in pairs successively. A pair of buffalos is led to opposite sides of the festival grounds and is made to stand near two flags called Ngu Phung. As soon as the right signal is released, the two buffaloes are led into the fighting circle. At the next signal, the two leaders release the ropes that are attached to the noses of the buffalos. With well-practiced movements, the buffalos rush into each other, using their fighting skills to decide the right to enter the next match while the spectators shout and urge the fighting along.

The winning buffalo goes to the next round till the final winner emerges. The matches varied in terms of time, depending on the strength and stamina of the buffalos. At the completion of the fight, the spectacle of "receiving the buffalos" is very interesting as the leaders must then catch the winning buffalo to grant it its reward.

In the villages, the preparations for participation in the buffalo fight event at Do Son Town event is an elaborate process. The preparations normally start from the 5th and the 6th lunar month. The competing buffalos are carefully selected and methodically trained for months in advance of the festival. Buffaloes of 4 to 5 years old with good appearance, wide chest, big groin, long neck, acute bottom and bow shaped horns are selected. Then qualifying or elimination rounds are held. The buffaloes finally selected for the fight in Do Son Town are fed in separate cages to keep them from contact with other buffaloes.

In recent years, Do Son Buffalo Fighting Festival attracted thousands of domestic and international tourists in addition to the local people. Buffalo fights and Bull fights are also held in Maghe Sankranti festival in Nepal. It is celebrated by the Nepalese on 1st Magh according to Vikrami calendar which normally befalls on 14th January.

Ok Om Bok Festival of Vietnam

The Khmer ethnic people of Mekong delta of Vietnam annually celebrate the Ok Om Bok Festival to revere their gratitude to the Moon Goddess for giving them rain, bumper harvest and rich aquatic resources. Worshiping the Moon Goddess for continuing such blessings is also obviously associated. The festival begins on a full moon day, normally on 14th or 15th October. The Moon Goddess is regarded as deity for crops and aquatic sources. In each village, the festival takes place on the yard of a local pagoda, and the whole province's celebration of the festival takes place at Ba Om Pond. The festival is also called as Cung Trang. The festivities of the festival are held for more than one days.

Ngo Boat Race is the most attractive event of Ok Om Bok Festival. This race is not only regarded as a game and a way to express the strength of consolidation of communities, but also as a traditional ritual to see off the God Water to the ocean after the growing season. Moreover, it is also considered as a religious ritual to commemorate the Snake God Nagar, who once turned into a lump of wood to help the Buddha cross the river.

During the night of the festival, a community feast is held in each of the villages at the vicinity of community pagoda. Green rice flakes, ripe bananas, sweet potatoes, coconuts, cake, fruit, and candy are the typical items offered to the Moon Goddess, and enjoyed in the feast.

Traditional games and traditional fashion shows are organised in the nights of the festival days. Flying lantern is the most archetypical game associated with the festival. Flying lantern is made with a bamboo frame pasted with paper. A kind of tinder is tied under the frame then fired, which makes the lantern fly high in the air. The flying lantern rises higher and higher in a mysterious and romantic breeze as if bringing the hopes and blessings from the Moon God.

Another interesting festivity of Ok Om Bok festival is construction of an archetypical bamboo gate. Two bamboo trunks are used to make the pillar of the gate while the coconut leaves are used to make the horizontal dome. The top of the gate is decorated with twisted betel leaves such that the gate symbolizes twelve months of the year. Moreover, seven split areca-nuts are placed at top of the gate in the shape of bee wings to symbolize seven days of the week.

Bung Bang Fai festival of Thailand

Bung Ban Fai or Rocket festival is celebrated with great pomp and magnificence mainly by Lao people in Yasothon province of Thailand. Traditionally, it was held to worship three deities to obtain enough rain for rice farming and to gain blessings for prosperity and happiness. These deities are called as Phaya, Thaen and Naga.

The festival is celebrated before planting of seedlings in rice cultivation - during May to June. At present, the Buddhist rituals are followed in the worshiping ritual. However, it is presumed that the festival has evolved from pre-Buddhist fertility rites - before the 9th century invention of black powder. There is no precise history of the festival, but some researchers believe that it is originated in Tai or Dai culture in China's Yunnan Province.

The main festivity of this festival is launching rockets at sky like missiles, called as Bang Fai. These skyrockets are gigantic black-powder bottle rockets. Such a rocket is launched from a bottle made of Bamboo culms called Bung. Thus, the name of the festival is Bung Ban Fai.

Each family launches the rockets with great important, and wishes that its rockets make the biggest bang or travel the furthest distance. At present competitions are organised amongst people in launching rockets. Prizes are given to the most successful launches. Buddhist monks are regarded to be the best rocket builders. Their rockets are based on age old traditional blueprints. Various marry making programmes are also obviously integral part of the festival. Party atmosphere continues for several days with music, dancing and boisterous partying.

Xen Xo Phon Festival of Vietnam

The Tai Don or White Tai people of Mai Chu region of Vietnam have been celebrating Xen Xo Phon Festival as an age old tradition. The basic purpose of the festival is associated with worshiping God(s) for obtaining rain for rice and vegetable cultivation.

The festival is held on fourth month of the Lunar calendar (between April and May) for seven days. Several rituals and festive activities are performed during in these days. One of the festive programmes is somewhat similar to Hunchari of Bohag Bihu: In the evenings of the festival days in each of the villages a group of youths make a circuit to the households of the village by singing songs, and each family offer certain offerings by following tradition.

Royal Ploughing Ceremony of Cambodia

This agrarian festival is celebrated in certain parts of Cambodia, Sri Laka, Thailand, Burma and India (Tamil Nadu) but in different names. In Cambodia, the Khmer people called it Preah Reach Pithi Chrot Preah Neangkol. The Sinhala or Sinhales of Sri Laka called it as Vap Magula. The Burmese called it as Lehtun Mingala. In Tamil Nadu, it is celebrated as Ponner Uzhuthal. The original Thai name of this festival is Raek Na Khwan. The meaning as well as purpose of the festival is quite obvious – auspicious and royal beginning of ploughing land for rice cultivation.

In Thailand, this festival has been celebrating since Sukhothai kingdom (1238-1438) while the Burmese chronicles traditionally attribute the start of this rite to the late 500s CE during the Pagan dynasty. It is interesting that in Thailand this festival has been combined with another festival by King Mongkut (1851 to 1868). The King Mongkut combined both the festivals into one and named as Phra Ratcha Phithi Phuetcha Mongkhon Charot Phra Nangkhan Raek Na Khwan.

Metemneo festival of Yimchunger tribe of Nagaland

Metemneo is the most significant festival of Yimchunger tribe of Nagaland. It is celebrated after harvesting Millet crop, and held normally in the second week of August for five days. Each day has specific name: Shito, Zhihdo, Zumdo, Khihresuk and Shiresuk respectively. Various deities are worshiped during the festival for thanksgiving and obtaining continuous blessings. Moreover, they do prayer for the souls of those who would die in the year. In addition to the religious rituals there are marked rituals to be performed on each day which are meant for socio-economic development of their villages and community. The rituals of this kind are as follows:

Day 1: **Shito: C**leaning of the village and repairing of village roads through collective action are carried out on this day.

Day 2: **Zhihdo :** The paths leading to the fields is improved, and disturbing landslides are repaired on this day.

Day 3: **Zumdo:** Repairing of inter-village roads is the main community work on this day.

Day 4: **Khihresuk** : On this day the water points and springs are cleaned.

Day 5: **Shiresuk** : The mandatory rituals of this day is cleaning and worshiping of agricultural tools.

The Metemneo festival is marked also by engagements between the young boys and girls. Other festivities include community feast, traditional dance-cum-music programme, inviting friends and guests, exchanging gifts, love and respect.

Monyu festival of Phoms

The Phoms tribe of Nagaland have 4 major agrarian folk festivals. These are – Monyu, Moha, Bongvum and Paangmo. Monyu is the most extensive and important among the four festivals. It is held after sowing seeds in Paddy field - normally in first week of April for 6 days. Each of the days has specific name, and on each day definite rituals or festivities are performed. The names and rituals of each of the days are briefly stated hereunder:

Day 1: **Shongten-Laiphen**: Overall preparation is done for celebrating the festival. Families in groups collect plantain leaves and bamboos for steaming food items. On this day, who do not own these plants in their farm are at liberty to collect from anyone else's farm without permission.

Day 2: **Aiha Okshok**: It is the day of feasting and marry making in different peer groups. Singing traditional songs and traditional dancing take place within peer groups in Murungs. Brewing of all kinds of rice beer is also part of the feasting. In fact, marry making in Manyu festival start from this day.

Day 3: **Chingi Okshok**: It is the day for family get together and family feasting. Every family slaughter at least one animal for the feast. One or more domestic animal is especially kept for the purpose. On this day married daughter with her spouse visit parents. An especial dish is prepared for them along with other traditional cuisines.

Day 4: **Yeindhu**: On this day relatives and guest from far and near come together to share love, reverence and gift. The word 'Yein' means guest. It is also the day of paying respect and adieu to departed souls jointly with relatives and friends.

Day 5: **Chingthem**: It is the most festive day of the festival. The community as whole celebrates by singing traditional songs, performing folk dance, drinking rice beer and playing traditional games. Men and women, young and old adorn themselves with colourful traditional attires. A big community feast is organised in which all participate.

Day 6: **Yeinyan**: It is the closing and dispersal day of the festival. Beating of log drum takes place in all the morning. It is believed that all invited guests should leave the village before ending of the beating of log drum so that no bad luck would befall on them. The leftover meat and food items are preserved and cleaning activities are carried out. In night the young people feast together at the outskirts of the village.

In addition to those mentioned above, there would be beating of log drum during nights in every Morung of the village for two to three hours. The purpose of beating drum is to evoke blessings from God as well as to signal the celebration of Monyu to other neighbouring villages.

Aoling festival of Kanyak people of Nagaland

Aoling festival is celebrated by the Kanyak people of Nagaland after sowing seeds in Jhum field. Normally, it is held in first week of

April for 6 days. However, dates may differ among the villages. The basic purpose of the festival is to seek blessings of Yongwan, the supreme God so as to have a bountiful harvest in the upcoming agricultural year. The Kanyak people also regard it as their New Year festival. They identify this festival with the blooming of the red Coral tree flowers and red lilies, and thus regarded also as jubilant spring festival. Each of the 6 days of the festival has specific name. There are definite rituals and festive activities to be observed in each of the days.

The first 3 days are called Hoi Lah Nyih, Yin Mok Pho Nyih and Mok Shek Nyih respectively. These three days are meant for preparatory activities of the festival. Each family finishes weaving of traditional cloths and prepare traditional foodstuff and rice beer for the festival. Organisers collect animals and other materials from the families for the community feast.

The fourth day is called as Lingnyu Nyih. This day is meant for marry making - dancing, singing and feasting as a community. In the community feast, an archetypical cuisine is specially prepared by steaming Nyuk-nye (a kind of sticky rice) in clay pots. Meat is cooked in abundance in different styles and Yu-shei (rice beer) is enjoyed abundantly. The men perform war dances wearing their headgears adorned with hornbill feathers and boar's tusks, and brass skull necklaces. Gun-firing with real gunpowder takes place as part of celebration which creates a distinctive ambiance for the festival, and is symbolic of the glory of the headhunting days of the Konyaks.

The final two days' are called Lingha Nyih and Lingshan Nyih. The ritualistic activities of these two days bear great significance for family wellbeing, community cohesiveness and social development. Both the days are dedicated to spend time with family and cleaning the whole village and also individual houses.

Dree festival of Apatani people of Arunachal Pradesh

Dree festival is celebrated by the Apatani people who inhabit in Ziro valley of Arunachal Pradesh. Apatani people are famous for their unique practices of wet rice cultivation and sustainable agricultural techniques. They traditionally observe a series of agrarian festivals starting from the sowing to the harvesting of wet rice cultivation with the purpose of obtaining blessings of various deities for bumper yield. The main agrarian folk festivals are Chandii, Tamu, Dree, and Yahung. The Chandi and Tamu festivals are observed during the sowing period. Yahung festival is observed just before the harvest. Dree festival is observed during growing period of crop, and it is celebrated most extensively and magnificently.

Dree festival is celebrated for three days. Five deities namely, Tamu, Metii, Medvr, Mepin and Danyi are worshiped by sacrificing domestic fowls, animals and eggs. The deities are worshiped for five different kinds of benefits mentioned below:

- ➢ Tamu is worshiped to ward off the insects and pests.

- ➢ Metii is worshiped to ward off epidemics and other ailments of the human beings.

- ➢ Medvr is worshiped for elimination of unfavourable elements from crop field. A purification ritual is performed to cleanse the agricultural fields.

- ➢ Mepin is worshiped to seek blessings for healthy crops and wellbeing of mankind.

- ➢ Danyi is worshiped for sustainable fertility of the soil, abundance of aquatic lives in the rice fields, healthy cattle and for prosperity of all human beings.

In addition to the religious rituals, the festival community feast, traditional cuisines, folk dance and folk music are marked festivities of Dree festival. The traditional songs and dance associated with this festival is called as Daminda. The festive customs of the pre-celebration starts one day before the main festival. Offering Cucumber to one and all in the community feast is a typical ritual observed. Apatani people regard Cucumber as divinity of vegetables, and boon for bountiful- fertile agriculture.

Sohrai festival of Santal, Prajapati etc.

Sohrai festival is primarily celebrated by the Santal, Prajapati, Kurmi, Munda and Orang people inhabit in different parts of India particularly in Jharkhand, Bihar, Chhattisgarh, Odisha and West Bengal. It is celebrated after harvest of paddy crop during October or November. The dates vary among the places coinciding with harvest of the crop. At present, January 12 is the declared holiday for Sohrai festival in Jharkhand. Moreover, the festival is also celebrated according to Solar calendar and starts a day after starting on the day of Amavaya in the month of Kartik.

Most of the rituals of this festival are by large similar to rituals of Magh Bihu. Traditionally, the festival is celebrated for 3 days or 5 days in different localities. Santals call each of the 3 days in specific name, and observe specific rituals on each day. First day is Um-Hiloah, second day is Takai-Hiloah, and the third day is Addako-Hiloah. The main rituals observed are as hereunder:

➤ The ritual of the first day of the festival begins with Goth Puja in grazing land of cattle. Goth means. Grazing ground of cattle. Goth Puja is performed by Naike (the priest of the village) along with the menfolk of the village. As a part of the Puja, a feast is enjoyed by the menfolk and Naike with Khichuri and rice beer. All the items of the feasts first offered to the deities particularly to the deity called as Marun buru. On completion of the feast, the leftover Khichuri is then distributed to every family of the village on leaves of Banyan tree. All the ingredients of this feast are collected from the families of the community or village. In some localities the feast is arranged with the rice, fowl and rice beer.

➢ In the afternoon of Um-Hiloah day an egg is laid on the path to the village by which bullocks and buffalo return homes from grazing land. The owner of the bullock or buffalo which stamps on the egg will gift a pot of rice beer in the forthcoming festival of the village.

➢ On the day of Takai-Hiloah, the second day of the festival, the cattle are bathed, and their horn and foreheads are anointed with vermilion diluted in oils. Garlands made by strewing paddy strands are tied across their foreheads. In some localities colourful drawing are made on the bodies of the cattle. Moreover, a special traditional food prepared from 7 definite ingredients is offered to the cattle. In the night of this day, earthen lamps are lighten by every family at cattle sheds, courtyard, kitchen and garden, and worship the deity of animals Gaurea or Pasupati or Bongas. After the worship, Prasad is distributed among the household members and neighbours.

➢ An indigenous ritualistic art form known as Sohrai art is carried out by the women with the inherent purpose of welcoming the harvest and entertaining the cattle on the second day. In this art form in each family, women clean the house, coat the wall with a layer of white mud, and decorate the walls with various types of murals and fingertips.

➢ On Addako-Hiloah, the third day the cattle shed is cleaned and worshiped. At night a community feast is organised as closing event of the festival. Moreover on this day, the married daughter with spouse visits her parents' home. Especial traditional dishes are especially prepared for them. Exchange of love, respect and gifts takes place between both the families.

Santal, Prajapati, Kurmi, Munda and Orang are aboriginal groups of people in various parts of India and are Austroasiatic people. The rituals and festivities of performed in the festival by different tribes and localities are similar in nature but not exactly the same.

Hareli Festival of Chhattisgarh

Hareli is the main festival of the Gond tribe who primarily inhabit in the state of Chhattisgarh. The word Hareli means vegetation or greenery. The festival is celebrated once the rice field becomes green with the luxuriant crop - generally falls on the months of July and August. Of course, at present people celebrate it on fixed date – on the day of Shravan Amavasya. The basic purpose of this day long festival is to worship Goddess Kutki Dai, the deity of the crops so as to have good yields. Majority of the rituals of this festival are quite similar to some of the rituals of Bihu festivals.

➢ Bullocks and cows are washed, paid reverence, and fed especial traditional foodstuff.

➢ Farm implements are cleaned and kept tidily in proper place.

➢ The leaves and branches of the Bhelva tree are planted on the fields with the belief that the branches reduce pests attack.

➢ The entrance of the houses is adorned by hangings branches of Neem tree. The ITK associated with this ritual is that the branches of Neem tree purifies the air, keeps insects away and helps in the prevention of several diseases.

➢ Children play a traditional game called as Gedi. In this game the players get ascended to big bamboo sticks and move around the fields.

> Traditional cuisines of medicinal value are enjoyed in the festival which are prepared from selected vegetables. Most popular cuisines are Kanda bhaji, Kochai patta, Chowlai bhaji, Lal bhaji, Bohar bhaji and Kohda.

> Muthiya rolls, Angarkar roti, Chousera roti are some of the special preparations that are made with rice flour.

> An archetypical meal called as Bore-basi is prepared by dipping rice in curd, water or buttermilk. It is beneficial to bear with heat, and thus resembles to Poita-Bhat rejoiced in Bohag Bihu.

> The main traditional sweet items prepared in the festival are Doodh fara, Bidiya, Bafauli, Kusli, Khurmi and Balooshahi.

Puthari festival of Karnataka

Puthari or Huttari festival is celebrated in Kodagu district in the state of Karnataka at the occasion of starting harvesting of Paddy crop. The word Puthari comes from Puth -Ari meaning new-rice. The festival is held for a week. It befalls in Kodava month of Birchayar calendar (November or December) as Paddy is normally harvested in the region in this period. However, in North Malabar region of the state it is celebrated in the Leo month of Birchayar calendar (around September) as Paddy is harvested there in this period.

Puthari festival begins on full Moon-day. The exact date and time of beginning of the festival is decided by priest. The festival starts with religious rituals performed at the temple of Padi Igguthappa. The other main rituals and festivities are as hereunder:

> Houses are cleaned and painted before Puthari.

> A special dessert called Thambutt is prepared from rice flour and mashed bananas.

➢ In the afternoon of the first day, a ritual called as Nere-Kattivo is held in which leaves of certain trees are tied together and placed on a mat. These are called Nere. Nere-Kattivo ritual is followed by the ceremony of cutting paddy sheaves called as Kad-Edpo ceremony. In each village people in group go to the fields in colourful traditional attires in a procession. A woman carries a lamp in front of the procession. The eldest man of each family cuts an odd number of paddy sheaves and hands them over to other family members. At the time of cutting sheaves they sing 'Poli Poli Deva' means 'May we prosper, O God!'.

➢ The group then head back to the houses with the sheaves in hands. The sheaves are then kept before the prayer lamp in respective homes. The youngsters then tie the Nere at prominent places in the house.

➢ A community feast is held at the night. Firecrackers are burst later in the night.

➢ On the second day, the Mane Paado ceremony takes place in which two or four singers with traditional hourglass drums go from house to house of the hamlet and sing and beat the drums The songs are mostly sing to praises the members of the family. They are followed by youngsters. It continues till last day of the festival.

➢ In the evening of last day of the festival, people go to a selected greenery called as the Mand, and perform traditional dance called a Kolatta which is popularly known as Dandiya.

GLOSSARY

Sl. No	Term	Meaning
1	Agoli-kolpat	The front part of a banana leaf.
2	Amroli-porua	Weaver ant (red)-Oecophylla smaragdina. Also called as Red ant.
3	Axomiya	Refers to Assamese race or Assamese language
4	Bajna	Synonym of Bandish
5	Bandish	The word Bandish is a term used in Hindustani music: "A composition in Raga music. This term is broadly used for any type of composition in Hindustani Art music- even rhythmic compositions are referred as Bandish".
6	Bichani	A traditional tool made from thin sticks of Bamboo, Cane or Tora(Alpinia nigra) used as a manually operated fan.
7	Bihubadya	The typical musical instruments accompanied with Bihunach and Bihunam are called as Bihubadya. The term is used in this book to mean one or all the instruments. The Bihubadya are Bihu-dhol, Mohor-xingor-penpa(Gutia Penpa and Juria Penpa), Toka (Haat-toka and Mati-toka), Gogona and Xutuli, Pati-tal and Baanhi.
8	Bihu-competitions	Refers to the competitions organised in the Bihutoli of present era. The various Bihu-competitions include Hunchari, Jeng Bihu, Bihuwati, Bihuwa, Bihunach, Bihunam, Dhol-badon, Penpa-badon, Koni-junj, Pitha-pona, Assamese traditional constumes.
9	Bihu-culture	Bihu-culture refers to all cultural aspects, components and resources related the Bihu festivals in totality.
10	Bihu festivals	Refers to three agrarian folk festivals of Assamese people which include Bohag Bihu, Magh Bihu and Kati Bihu.
11	Bihugeet	Synonym of Bihunam.
12	Bihunach	The prototypical dance form associated with Bohag Bihu.
13	Bihunam	The prototypical songs associated with Bohag Bihu.
14	Bihutoli	In present era, as part celebrating Bohag Bihu, cultural functions are organised. Such cultural functions are of 1 to 3 days duration, and called in several names such as Bihutoli, Bihu-sanmilan, Bihu-utshav, Basanta-mela and Basanta-utsav. In this book the term Bihutoli is used to mean such a cultural function. The word is used for both singular and plural meanings.

Sl. No	Term	Meaning
15	Bihuwa	Bihuwa means a boy or man who participates in Hunchari and/or Bihu-competitions. Bihuwa also means a boy or man who performs Bihunach, sings Bihunam, and/or plays Bihubadya. The word is used for both singular and plural meanings.
16	Bihuwan	Bihuwan is a specially woven prototypical scarf or towel like item of Assamese culture. The females present Bihuwan to dear ones and respected ones as special gift at the occasion of Bohag Bihu. The word is used for both singular and plural meanings.
17	Bihuwati	Bihuwati means a girl or woman who participates in Rati Bihu, Jeng Bihu and/or Bihu-competitions. Bihuwati also means a girl or woman who performs Bihunach, sings Bihunam, and/or plays Bihubadya. The word is used for both singular and plural meanings.
18	Bol	"Words or syllables implied in Taala. The term also means syllables of instruments – it may be percussion, string or wind instruments or the syllables in a song"
19	Bota	Bota is a kind of exquisite traditional utensils of Assamese culture. Generally made of bell-metal but also made from cane and wood too. It is a daily used utensil in which mainly Tamul-pan is offered. Bota is sometimes used instead of Xorai to offer Guwapan etc. to the God and respected ones.
20	Chaat	The term Chaat is associated with the rituals of 'washing bullocks and cows' in Bohag Bihu. It refers to 3 things related to the rituals. A simple tool made from a piece bamboo strip of about 2 inches breath and 1.5 feet length by creating 2 to 5 numbers of spokes. Slices of vegetables are stitched with its spoke so as to use to throw the slices on bullocks and cows. The tool with stitched slices of vegetables is also called as Chaat. The slices of vegetables used to throw on bullocks and cows are also called as Chaat. All the materials including slices of vegetable and medicinal paste etc. together are also called as Chaat.
21	Dola	Dola is a big sized round shaped bamboo-made utensil of Assamese culture.

Sl. No	Term	Meaning
22	Dholar-cheu	When a definite set of bols is played in a definite construction and rhythm(s) in Bihu-dhol, the Bandish so produced is called as Dholar-cheu. The term is used for both singular and plural meanings.
23	Duchaporia Chapori	Duchaporia Chapori refers to two consecutive claps in a typical rhythm in which Bihunam are sung.
24	Gamosa	Gamosa is same with Bihuwan as an item - a prototypical scarf or towel like item of Assamese culture. It is used by Assamese people for various purposes, particularly as towel and as muffler. At present it is also used to felicitate personalities in meetings etc. It is so archetypal that currently some people consider it as a kind of symbolic piece of costume to reveal cultural identity as Axomiya(Assamese people). The process of obtaining GIS for Gamosa is in progress.
25	Gutia-penpa	The Mohor-xingor-penpa of one horn is called Gutia-penpa or Ahingia-penpa
26	Hanchati	A prototypical handkerchief
27	Juria-penpa	The Mohor-xingor-penpa of two horns is called Juria-penpa
28	Laru	Laru is a kind of round shaped sweet.
29	Penpa	Mohor-xingar-penpa is shortly called as Penpa
30	Penpar-cheu	When a definite set of *bols* is played in definite construction and rhythm(s) in Mohor-xingar-penpa, the Bandish so produced is called as Penpar-cheu.
31	Pitha	Pitha means flour. The typical cake or biscuit like items prepared from rice flour are also called as Pitha.
32	Seleng-sadar	Seleng-sadar is a specially woven prototypical costume of Assamese culture used by both menfolk and womenfolk in special occasions including of Bohag Bihu. It is also considered as an honorary piece of costume, and used as a special gift item to offer to respected persons in various occasions including Bohag Bihu.
33	Tongali	A prototypical costume of Assamese culture. It is wear by menfolk at waist. It is considered as an preferable costume of Bihuwa.
34	Xaat Bihu	Xaat Bihu refers to 7 days of celebration of Bohag Bihu. Each of the seven days has specific name and definite mandatory rituals to perform.

Sl. No	Term	Meaning
35	Xewa	Xewa is typical style of praying the God(s) and offering reverence to respected person or group by Hindu Assamese people. The prostration pose of Sastanga Pranam of Hinduism is followed in doing Xewa.
36	Xorai	Xorai is a kind of exquisite traditional utensils of Assamese culture. Generally made of bell-metal but also made from cane and wood too. It is mainly used to keep offerings in prayer to the God(s) or in conveying reverence to a person or group.
37	Yojona	When a verse of Bihunam is sung without beat is called as Yojona.

REFERENCES

1. Directorate for Welfare, Govt. of Assam (2020). List of Tea Garden at Assam.

2. Indian Tea Association (2017). Tea Growing Regions. pp. 1.

3. Ali, Salim and Daniel, J.C. (2002). The book of Indian Birds. Oxford University Press. pp. 6

4. Hem Barua (1973). The Bihu Festival. *Indian Literature* :Vol. 16, No. 3/4 : 35-43

5. http://en.wikipedis.org/wiki/Sankranti

6. http://www.xobdo.org/dic/ভাস্কৰাব্দ

7. https://peoplepill.com/people/kumar-bhaskara-varman/

8. https://templesinindiainfo.com/about-mesha-sankranti

9. https://astrobix.com/astrosight/202-uttarayan-and-dakshinayan.html

10. https://rgyan.com/en/festival-detail/astrological-significance

11. https://astrotalk.com/astrology-blog/makar-sankranti-2020-astrological-significance/

12. https://horoscope.astrosage.com/tula-sankranti-rituals-2020/

13. Cambridge English Dictionary. Definition of Ritual.

14. Bell, Catherine (1997). Ritual: Perspectives and Dimensions. New York: Oxford University Press. pp. 138–69

15. Joost Van Itterbeeck et.al (2014). Indigenous Knowledge of the Edible Weaver Ant Oecophylla sma-ragdina Fabricius Hymenoptera. *Ethnobiology Letters* : January, 2014: 4

16. Werawich Pattarayingsakul (2017). Angiotensin-converting enzyme inhibitory and antioxidant peptides from digestion of larvae and pupae of Asian weaver ant, Oecophylla smaragdina, Fabricius. *Journal of the Science of Food and Agriculture* : 97(10):3133-3140

17. Zelman Kathleen (2019). Food and Nutrition: Bugs You Can Eat. *OnHealth* : January 29, 2019: 5

18. Vidhu, V.V. and Evans, D. A. (2015). Ethnoentomological values of Oecophylla smaragdina (Fabricius). *Current Science*:109(3):572-579

19. Joost Van Itterbeeck *et.al.* (2014). *Ethnobiology Letters* : January, 2014: 4

20. Werawich Pattarayingsakul (2017). *Journal of the Science of Food and Agriculture* : 97(10):3133-3140

21. Zelman Kathleen (2019). Food and Nutrition: Bugs You Can Eat. *OnHealth*: January 29, 2019: 5

22. Swarganga Music Foundation (2004). Glossary database list definitions for different terms used in Indian classical music. pp. 2

23. Monier-Williams, Monier (1899). A Sanskrit-English Dictionary, London: Oxford University Press.

24. Nettl, Bruno; Ruth M. Stone; James Porter; Timothy Rice (1998). The Garland Encyclopedia of World Music: South Asia: the Indian subcontinent. Routledge, ISBN 978-0-8240-4946-1

25. Swarganga Music Foundation (2004). Glossary database list definitions for different terms used in Indian classical music. pp. 2

26. Arangua, Michael (2020). What are the different types of love? Betterhelp: September 10, 2020: 3-4

27. Lochtefeld, James (2002). The Illustrated Encyclopaedia of Hinduism, Vol. 1: A-M, Rosen Publishing, ISBN 0-8239-2287-1. pp. 140

28. Mahanta, Khogen (2007). In Neog, Pradip (2014), Rangali Bihu Sanskriti. pp. 45.

29. Bhagawati, Ananda Mohon (1983). In Neog, Pradp (1987). Rongali Bihur Nitya Geet. pp 97

30. Bihu Surashya Sommitty, Assam(2011). Bihu Surashyar Niyamawali. pp. 13-15

31. Rajkhowa, Priyanka (2017).The Jewellery Art of Assam. *Northeast-Today*: August, 2017.

32. Taher, Mohammad (1993), "The Peopling of Assam and contemporary social structure", in Ahmad, Aijazuddin (ed.), Social Structure and Regional Development, New Delhi: Rawat Publication, pp. 201–218

33. Borgohain, Jatindra Kumar (2007). Asamar Sanskitik Itihas. Assam Sahitya Sabha, pp. 58.

34. Sir Edward Gait (1962). A History of Assam, 2nd edition 1962. page 2

35. Das, Paromita (2005). "The Naraka Legends, Aryanisation and the "varnasramadharma" in the Brahmaputra Valley". Proceedings of the Indian History Congress. Indian History Congress. 66: 224–230. JSTOR 44145840

36. Statement. Censusindia.gov.in. Archived from the original *on 6 February 2012. In* https://en.wikipedia.org/wiki/Assamese_language

37. Goswami, G. C.; Tamuli, Jyotiprakash (2003), "Asamiya", in Cardona, George; Jain, Dhanesh (eds.), The Indo-Aryan Languages, Routledge, pp. 391–443. In https://en.wikipedia.org/wiki/Assamese

38. Guha, Amalendu (1983). The Ahom Political System: An Enquiry into the State Formation Process in Medieval Assam (1228-1714). *Social Scientist*: 11 (12): 3–34. In https://en.wikipedia.org/wiki/

39. Buragohain, Homendra Nath (2019). Bihur Otit, Bortoman aru Amar Sanskritik Parampara. *Xaatbihu* (Souveniour), ed. Indrani Gogoi, pp. 135

40. Eric Hoffer (2006), The Passionate State of Mind: And Other Aphorisms: Hopewell Publications, LLC (January 2006),

41. Changmai Nitul (2016). Bihur Itihah aru Parampora. Students' Stores. Pp. 27

42. Goswami Pallabpran(2019). Moimat Senimaik Bichari. *Senimai*(Souveniour): pp 106

43. Hussain Ismail (2013). Rongali Bihur Prasang-koksh, Jyoti Prakashan, pp. 110

44. Changmai Nitul (2016). Bihur Itihah aru Parampora. Students' Stores. pp. 27

45. Ronald E Riggio (2017). Are We All Becoming More Self-centred? *Psychology Today*: July 27, 2017.

46. Wendell Berry (2002). The Art of the Commonplace: The Agrarian Essays. In https://www.goodreads.com/work/quotes

47. Thomas, G. and Patrick, W. (1978). Introduction to Philosophy Messer. George Allen & Unwin ltd, London. pp. 146

48. Saikia, Anil (2019). Krama-bikashot Rongali Bihu, *Xaatbihu*: 45-46

49. Sonowal, Tilu (2019). Bohag Bihur Utpatti aru Sonowal Bohag Bihu, *Xaatbihu* :67

50. Bihu Kristi Charcha aru Bikash Sammitti, Jorhat (1987). Rangali Bihur Bibhinna ProtiyogitarArhimulak Niyanawali. Ed. Prabir Dutta. pp. 8.

51. Jovel, K. V. R. Jovel et.al (2009). Modernization and culture loss: A natural experiment among native Amazonians in Bolivia Tsimane' - Amazonian Panel Study Working Paper. pp. 52

52. Turino Thomas (2008). Music as Social Life: The Politics of Participation. University of Chicago Press. In https://press.uchicago.edu/

53. Neog, Pradip (2013). Bihur Maryada Rakhyat Xanlista Xokolu Pakhyai Gurutta Diyak, *Prantik*: 16 – 31 March, 2020: 41-43

54. Green, T. A. (1997).Folklore: An Encyclopedia of Beliefs, Customs, Tales, Music, and Art. Calinfornia: ABC-CLIO, Inc. (1997)

55. Neog, Pradip (2013). Chinnamul Bihu Protiyogita, *Prantik*: 01-16 April, 2013: 21-25

56. Hem Barua (1973). The Bihu Festival. Indian Literature Vol. 16, No. 3/4: 35-43

57. Manger Amit (2015). Understanding Modernization and Cultural Resistance in Sikkim: A Sociological Analysis of Folk Music. Int. Res. J. Social Sci. : 4(5), 59-6659

58. Hussain Ismail (2013). Rongali Bihur Prasang-koksh. Jyoti Prakashan. pp. 110

59. Prafulladutta Goswami (1957). Bihu songs of Assam. Lawyers Book Stall. In http://www.asiafinebooks.com

60. Hussain Ismail (2013). Rongali Bihur Prasang-koksh. Jyoti Prakashan, pp. 110

61. Gandhia, Joykanta (1997). Hunchari Mukali Bihu Aru Bihunach. Bonolata, pp

62. Sarma, Nabin Chandra (1989). Axomiya Loka-Sanskritir Abhash. Bani Prokash. pp. 267.

63. Mohubulla, S. (2005). Amar Sanskritir Reh-Rup. *Bohagi* (Souveniour), ed.Mina Kumari Raimedhi: 216.

64. Chetia Tokheswar (2005). Bohag Bihu – Youvan aru Krishi Prajonanar Loka-Sanskriti, *Sadin- Basanta Sambhar*: 16.

65. Hem Barua (1973). The Bihu Festival. *Indian Literature* Vol. 16, No. 3/4: 35-43

66. Gogoi, Dinesh (2016). Bihu r Geet aru Namot Itihahar Jilikani, *Borgos* (Souvenir), ed. Prasanta Madhab Bora: 75

67. Neog, Pradip (2008). Bihu Binandia. Jyoti Prakashan. pp. 36-37

68. Gogoi, Lila(1969). Bihu Ati Samikhya. Banalata. pp. 37

69. Gogoi, Boun Thon (2019). Bihu Utshavar logot Jorita Keitaman Anushan, Sobda aru Bhabartha *Xaatbihu* :31

70. Gandhiya, Joykanta (1997). Hunchari: Mukali Bihu Aru Bihunach. Bonolata, pp. 22

71. Syam, Lalit (2019). Tai Syan Boudha Janagostir Jatiya Usav aru iar Samanayoir dikx. *Xaatbihu* :37

72. Saikia, Nagen (2017). Axomiya Manuhor Itihah. pp.330

73. Sarma, Nabin Chandra (1989). Axomiya Loka-Sanskritir Abhash. Bani Prokash. pp. 267

74. Goswami, P. (1966). The Springtime Bihu of Assam. In Axomiya Loka-Sanskritir Abhash. pp. 267

75. Bhattacharyya, T. (2005). Bishnupadi Sankranti, Bihu aru Alberuni, *Prantik* :01-16 April, 2005: 14

76. Tony Coolidge (2016) A Colourful Celebration of Life's Abundance: Amis Harvest Festival. http://www.culturalsurvival. org/news

77. 77.https://en.wikipedia.org/wiki/Amis_harvest_festivals

78. Surapon Nesusin(2019) Music of Nyah kur Enthnic group in Chaiyaphum province Journal of Fine and Applied Arts: Vol. 10 No. 2: pp. 92-111

79. Southeast Asian Languages:Mon Khmer languages project

80. https://travel.gaijinpot.com/otaue-rice-planting-festival/

81. https://vietnamdiscovery.com/hai-phong/activities/do-son-buffalo-festival/

82. Rachel Tran (2020). Ok Om Bok Festival: the Full Moon Festival in Mekong Delta. https://vietnamdiscovery.com/mekong-delta/activities/ok-om-bok-festival/

https://en.wikipedia.org/wiki/Rocket_Festival

83. Srisupun P. and Apichartwallob Y. (2009). Rocket Festival in Transition: Rethinking 'Bun Bangfai' in Isan. Paper presented at 1st Annual International Graduate Research Conference on Social Sciences and Humanities", April 2-3, 2009 at Bangkok.

84. https://www.tripsavvy.com/favorite-festivals-in-vietnam/

85. https://www.tourismcambodia.com/tripplanner/events-in-cambodia/royal-ploughing.htm

86. https://en.wikipedia.org/wiki/Phom_Naga

87. Emn(2015).Significance of the Phom Monyiu festival. Eastern Mirror : March 29: 2015

88. https://konyaktearetreat.com/event/along-festival/

89. https://www.india.com/travel/articles/what-to-expect-at-the-aoling-festival-of-nagaland-3625648/

90. https://www.tourmyindia.com/states/nagaland/metumniu-festival.html

91. https://www.indianetzone.com/82/metemneo_festival.htm

92. http://myarunachal.weebly.com/dree-festival.html

93. https://en.wikipedia.org/wiki/Sohrai

94. Indrajit Roychoudhury (2015) Sohrai: A Festival with Art. Indrosphere: Nov. 15, 2015 https://indroyc.com/2015/11/11/sohrai-a-festival-of-santhal-tribe/

95. Express News Service (2018). Santhals look forward to Sohrai: The News Indian Express 05th November 2018

96. https://beautyspotsofindia.com/hareli-festival/

97. https://www.evolveback.com/coorg/puthari-the-harvest-feast/

98. Neog, Pradip (2008). Bihu Binandia. Jyoti Prakashan. pp.

99. Begum Sofika and Gogoi Rajib (2006). Herbal recipe prepared during Bohag or Rongali Bihu in Assam. Indian Journal of Traditional Knowledge : 6(3):2007 pp.417-422

100. Hussain Sadiqul (2018). 101 herbs and trees of Assam. https://youtu.be/xHz2RUJ3QJM

APPENDICES

Appendix: I

Salient Rituals of Bohag Bihu

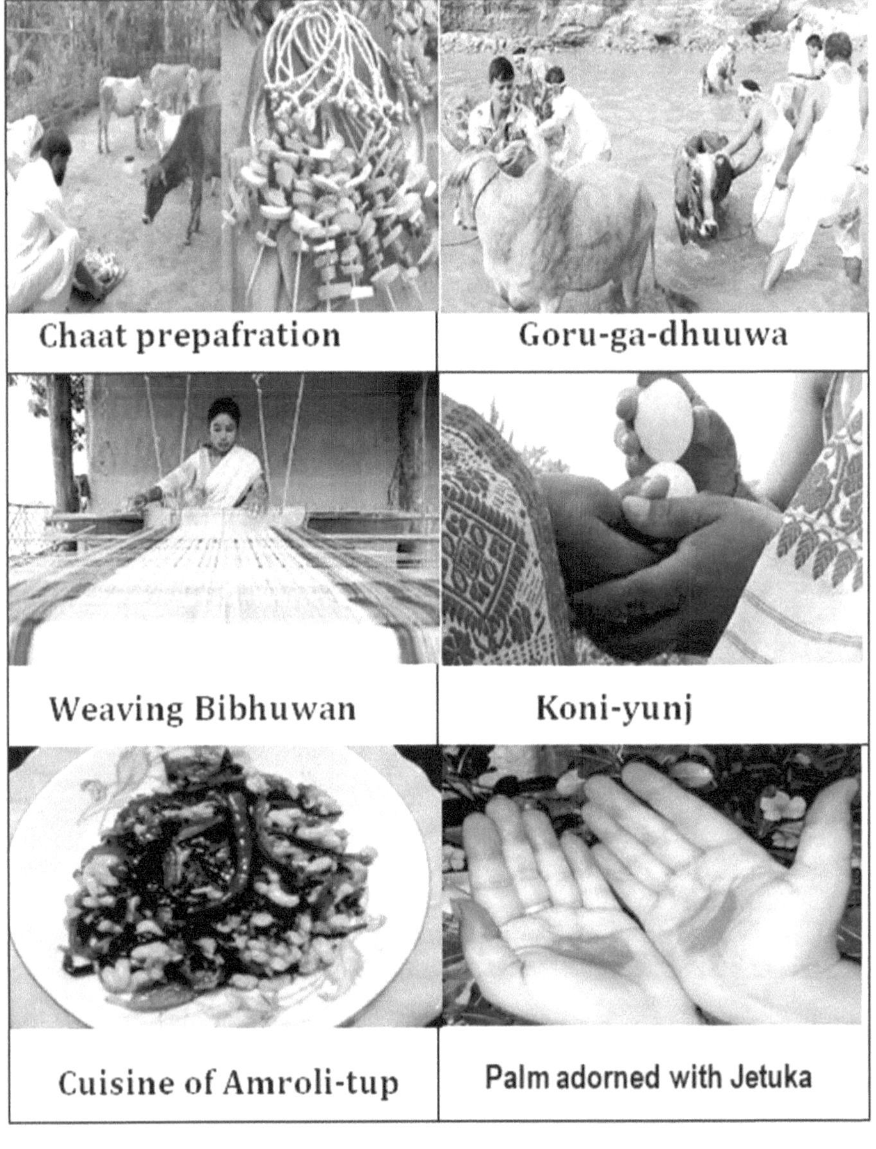

Chaat prepafration	Goru-ga-dhuuwa
Weaving Bibhuwan	Koni-yunj
Cuisine of Amroli-tup	Palm adorned with Jetuka

Appendix: II

Salient Rituals of Magh Bihu and Kati Bihu

Pitha-pona	Community feast + Bhelaghar
Mezi	Community fishing
Moh-yunj	Lighting Chaki in Kati Bihu

Appendix: III

Special items associated with Bihu festivals

Kopouphul

Keteki Phul

Kuli Sorai (Male+Female)

Keteki Soroi

Xorai

Bota

Appendix: IV

Rati Bihu and Jeng Bihu (Acrylic pictures)

Rati Bihu

Jeng Bihu

Appendix: V

Hunchari at courtyards of households

Hunchari by Bihuwa

Hunchari by Bihuwa and Bihuwati

Appendix: VI, a
Bhangima of Bihuwati's Bihunach

Appendix: VI, b

Bhangima of Bihuwati's Bihunach (cont...)

Appendix: VII

Bihubadya

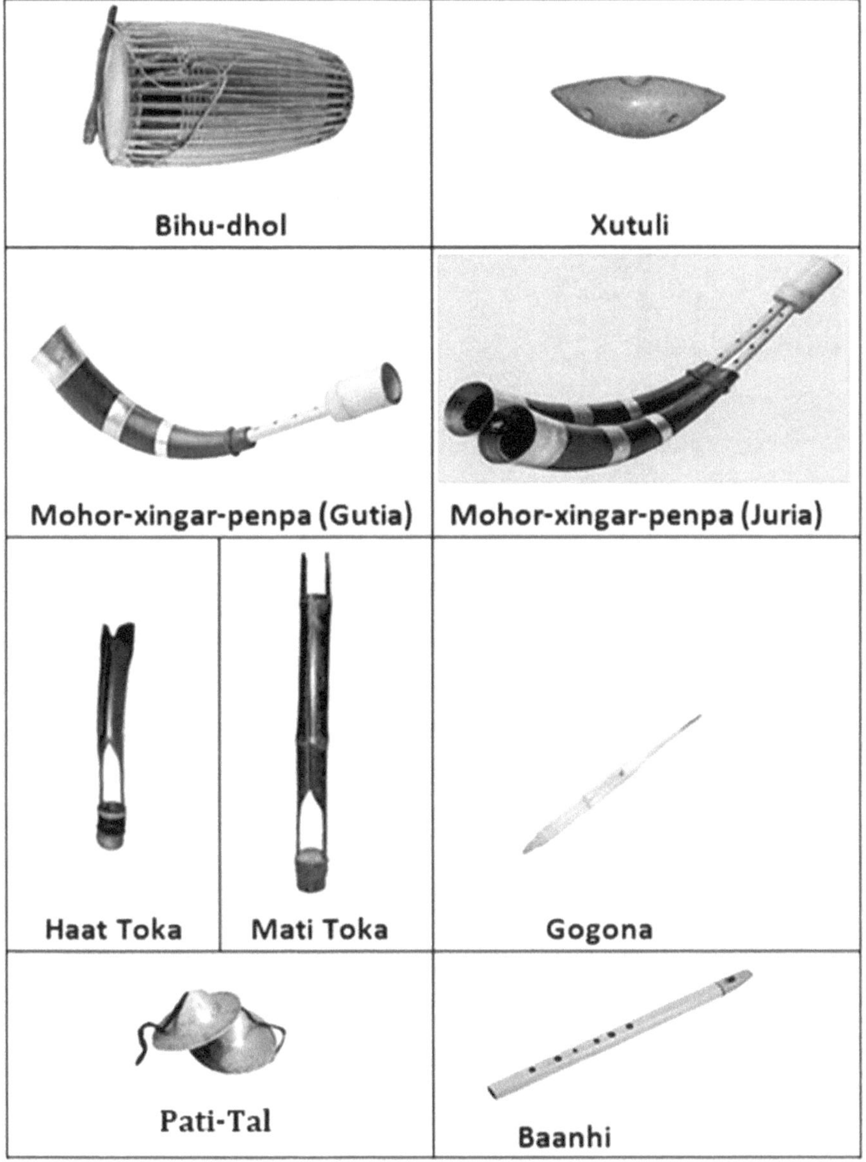

Appendix: VIII
Parts of Bihu-dhol and Mohor-xingal-penpa

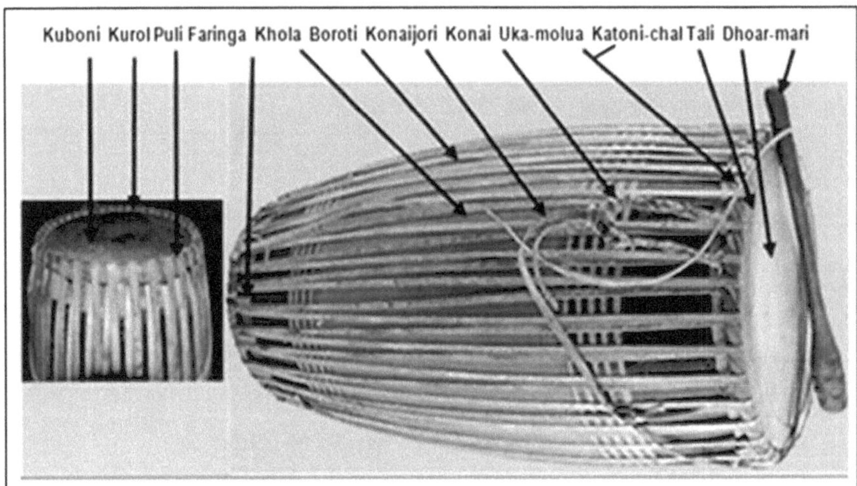

12 parts of Bihu-dhol

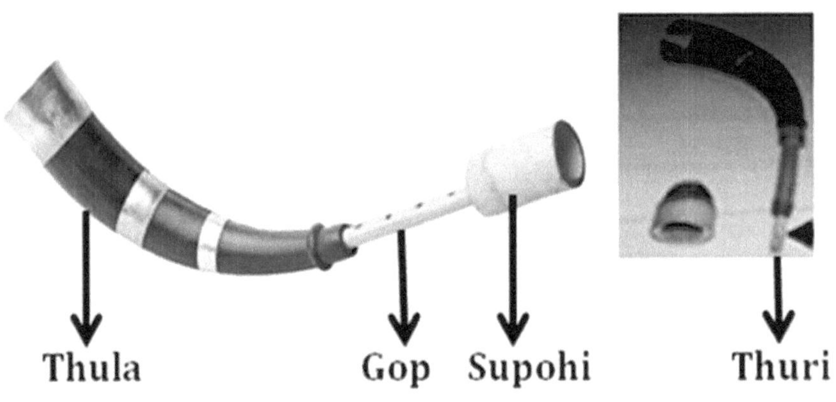

Parts of Mohor-xingar-penpa

Appendix: IX, a

Assamese ornaments

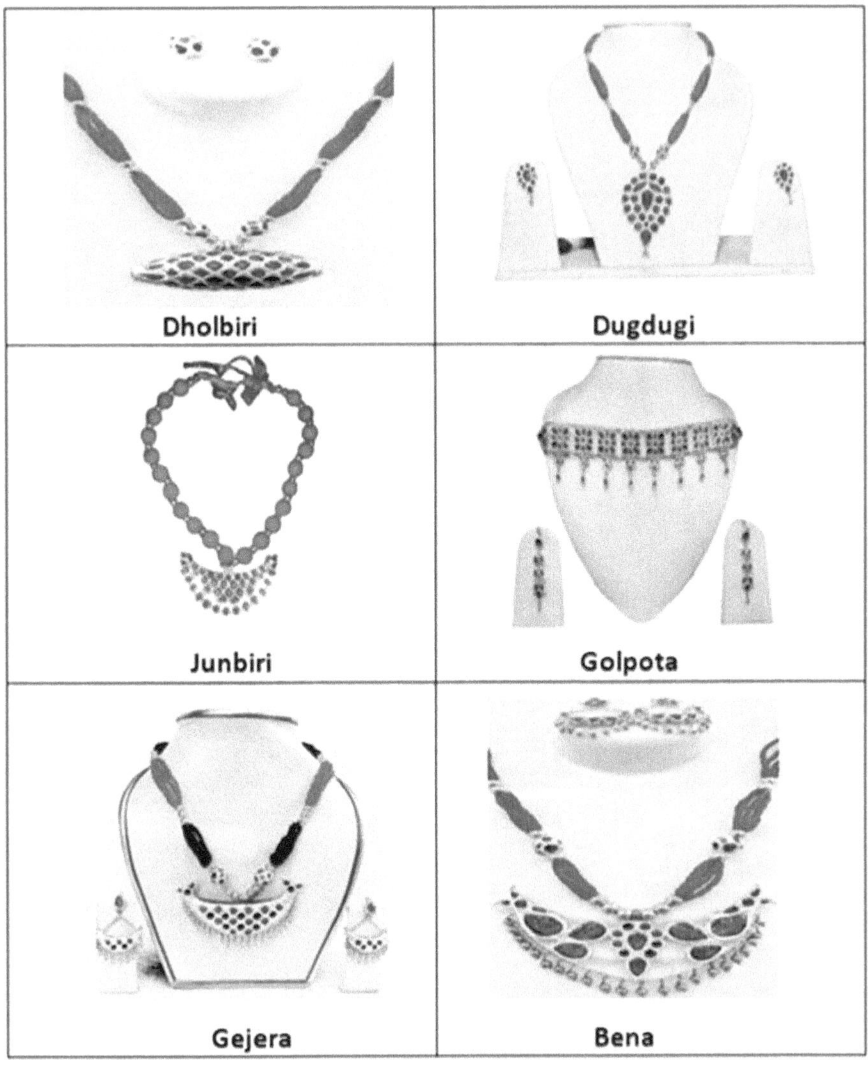

Appendix: IX, b

Assamese ornaments (Cont....)

Appendix: X,a
150 plant species for cuisine of 101 herbs of Bohag Bihu

1. Babori
(Chrysanthemum
coronarium L.)

2.   Pati hunda
(Cinnamomum bejol-
ghota)

3.   Tez pat
(C. tamala Fr.)

4.   Nephaphu
(Clerodendrum
colebrookianum Walp.)

5. Nangal bhanga
(C. serratum)

6.   Dhopat tita
(C. viscosum Vent)

7.   Kochu
(Colocasia escule-
nta (L.) Schott)

8. Kona himolu
(Comme lina
benghalensis L.)

9.   Tita mora
(Corchorus capsularis L.)

Appendix: X,b
150 plant species for cuisine of 101 herbs of Bohag Bihu

10. Mahudi (Croton caudatus Geisel.)	11. Ronga lau (Cucurbita maxima Duch. Ex Lamk.)	12. Gakhiroti/ Dhudh bon (Euphorbia hirta L.)
13. Heloshi (Enhydra fluctuans Lour.)	14. Panarnawa (Boerhavia diffusa L)	15. Bet gaz (Calamus erectus Roxb.)
16. Kalmegh (Andrographis paniculata (Burm. f.) Wall. ex Nees)	17. Hati khutura (Amaranthus spinosus L.)	18. Pani khutura (A. philoxe roides (Mart.) Griseb)

Appendix: X,c
150 plant species for cuisine of 101 herbs of Bohag Bihu

19. Khutura (A. viridis L.)

20.   Tora (Alpinia nigra (Gaertn.) Burtt)

21. Lai jabori (Drymaria diandra Bl)

22. Keha raj (Eclipta prostrata L.)

23.   Goru khis (Duchesnea indica (Andr.) Focke)

24.   Sutiya lofa (Fagopyr um esculentum Moench.)

25.   Surat gas (Dendrocnide sinuata (Bl.) Chew)

26. Teteli (Tamarindus indica.)

27.   Makhioti (Flemingia strob elifera (L.) R. Br. ex Ait.)

Appendix: X,d
150 plant species for cuisine of 101 herbs of Bohag Bihu

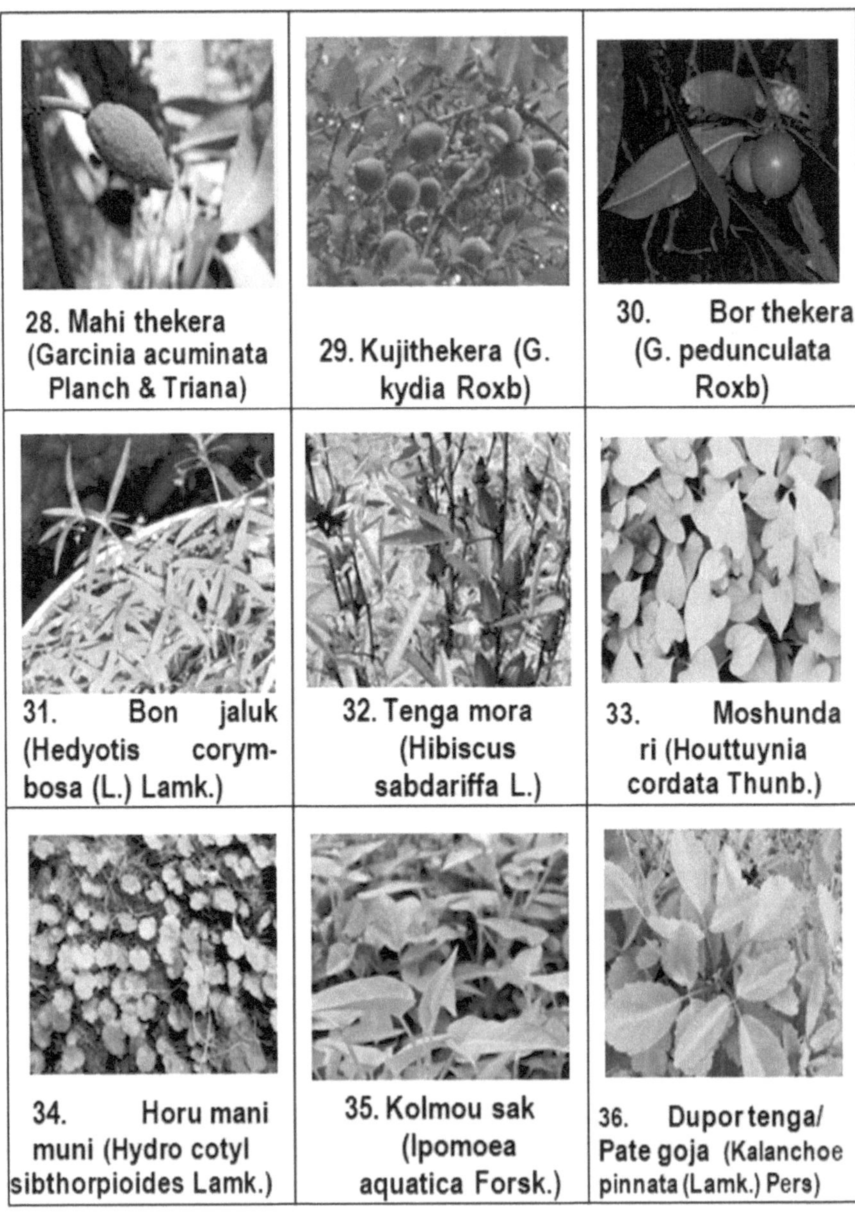

28. Mahi thekera (Garcinia acuminata Planch & Triana)

29. Kujithekera (G. kydia Roxb)

30. Bor thekera (G. pedunculata Roxb)

31. Bon jaluk (Hedyotis corymbosa (L.) Lamk.)

32. Tenga mora (Hibiscus sabdariffa L.)

33. Moshunda ri (Houttuynia cordata Thunb.)

34. Horu mani muni (Hydro cotyl sibthorpioides Lamk.)

35. Kolmou sak (Ipomoea aquatica Forsk.)

36. Dupor tenga/ Pate goja (Kalanchoe pinnata (Lamk.) Pers)

Appendix: X,e
150 plant species for cuisine of 101 herbs of Bohag Bihu

37. Kasi doriya (Lindernia ruelli-oides (Colsm.) Pen)

38. Digh loti (Litsea salicif olia (Roxb. ex Wall.) Hk. f.)

39. Kopou dhekia (Lygodi um flexuosum (L.) Sw.)

40. Beli poka (Melothria heter ophylla (Lour.) Cogn.)

41. Bioni sabota (Desmodi um gangeticum (L.) DC.)

42. Neuthoni (Por-tulaca grandi-flora Pollen D. Legrand)

43. Pani kachu (Sagittaria trifolia L.)

44. Pani Kola (Ottelia alis-moides (L.) Pers.)

45. Dhatura (Datura stramonium L.)

Appendix: X,f
150 plant species for cuisine of 101 herbs of Bohag Bihu

46. Bon jolokia /Bon-marich. (Clematis cadmia Bush.-ham.)	47. Nilakantha (Ecbolium ligu-strinum (Vahl) Vollesen)	48. Bok phool (Sesbania grandiflora Pers.)
49. Paleng (Spinacia oleracea L.)	50. Pirali Paleng (Talinum fruticosum L.)	51. Nilaji bon (Mimosa pudica)
52. Dhunduli (Trichosa nthes cucumerina L.)	53. Dhania (Coriandrum sativum L.)	54. Bilahi (Lycopersicon esculentum Mill)

Appendix: X,g
150 plant species for cuisine of 101 herbs of Bohag Bihu

55. Tubuki lota (Stephania japonica (Thunb.) Miers.)

56. Poshotiya (Vitex negundo L.)

57. Tez moi (Zanthoxylum nitidum (Roxb.) DC.)

58. Bagh anchora (Smilax perfoliata lour.)

59. Agora (Urena lobata L.)

60. Hati bhekuri (S. torvum Sw.)

61. Pok mou/ Lach koshi (S. nigrum L.)

62. Tita bhekuri (Solanum indicum L.)

63. Meshangi (Sarc och lamys pulcherrima Gaud.)

Appendix: X,h
150 plant species for cuisine of 101 herbs of Bohag Bihu

64. Jetuli poka (Rubus ellipticus Smith.)	65. Thereju tenga (Prunus jenkinsii Hk. f. & Th.)	66. Hahthengia / Malbhug khutura (Portulaca oleracea L.)
67. Modhu huleng (Polygonum chinense)	68. Bon jaluk (Oldenlandia corymbosa L.).	69. Hukloti (Pogostemon benghalense (Burm.f.)Kuntz.)
70. Singa pat (Plantago erosa Wall.)	71. Arani pan (P. hamiltonii DC.)	72. Pipolee (Piper longum L.)

Appendix: X,i
150 plant species for cuisine of 101 herbs of Bohag Bihu

73. Tita phul (Phlogacanthus thyrs-iflorus (Roxb.) Nees)

74. Bhedai lota (Paederia foetida L.)

75. Bor tengeshi (O. debilis H. B. K. var. corymbosa (DC.) Lour.

76. Horu tengeshi (Oxalis corniculata L.)

77. Bon tulsi (Ocimum basilicum L.)

78. Bhet phul (Nymphaea nouchali Burm. f.)

79. Amlokhi (Phyllanthus emblica L.)

80. Sewali (Nyctanthes arbor-tristis L.)

81. Podum (Nelumbo nucifera Gaertn.)

Appendix: X,j
150 plant species for cuisine of 101 herbs of Bohag Bihu

82. Kol gas (Musa balbisiana Colla)	83.　　Norosingha (Murraya koenigii (L.) Spreng.)	84. Nuni (Morus indica L.)
85. Sojina (Moringa oleifera Lamk.)	. Anshu gas (Morinda angustifolia Roxb.)	87. Haru　　meteka (Monochoria hastata (L.)Solms.)
88. Bhat kerela (M. cochinc-hinensis (Lour.) Spreng.)	89.　　Tita kerela (Momordica charantia L.)	90. Podina (Mentha spicata L.)

Appendix: X,k
150 plant species for cuisine of 101 herbs of Bohag Bihu

91. Phutkola (Melastoma malabathricum L.)	92. Am (Mangifera indica L.)	93. Bhol (L. cylindrica (L.) M. Roemer)
94. Jika (Luffa acutangula (L.) Roxb.)	95. Modhuri (Psidium guajava L.)	96. Ada (Zingiber officinale Rosc.)
97. Alu (S. Tuberosum L.)	98. Bengana (S. melongena L.)	99. Til (Sesamum orientale L.)

Appendix: X,I
150 plant species for cuisine of 101 herbs of Bohag Bihu

100. Durun (Leucas plukenetii (Roth.) Spreng.)	101. Jetuka (Lawsonia inermis L.)	102. Seng mora (Lasia spinosa (L.) Thw.)
103. Jati lau (Lagenaria siceraria (Molina) Stadley)	104. Piyaz (Allium cepa L.)	105. Sal kuwari (Aloe vera (L.) Burm. f.)
106. Mati kaduri (Alternanthera sess-ilis (L.) R. Br. ex. DC.)	107. Bali bhotora / Jilmil (Cheno-podium album L.)	108. Bor mani muni (Cente lla asiatica (L.) Urban.)

Appendix: X,m
150 plant species for cuisine of 101 herbs of Bohag Bihu

109. Soriyah (Brassica nigra (L.) Koch.)	110. Lai sak (B. juncea (L.) Czern.)	111. Kothal (Artocarpus heter ophyllus Lamk.)
112. Kumura (Benincasa hispida (Thunb.) Cog)	113. Puroi sak (Basella alba L.)	114. Bholuka banh (Bambusa balcooa Roxb.)
5. Brahmi (Bacopa monnieri (L.) Pennell.)	116. Moha neem (Azadirachta indica A. Juss.)	117. Nohoru (A. sativum L.)

Appendix: X,n
150 plant species for cuisine of 101 herbs of Bohag Bihu

118. Halodhi (Curcuma longa L.)

119. Man dhoniya (Eryngium foetidum L.)

120. Dhekia (Diplazium escu lentum(Retz.)Sw.)

121. Ou tenga (Dillenia indica L.)

122. Nol tenga (Tetra stigma leucostaphylum)

123. Suka (Rumex acetosa)

124. Morolia (Stellaria media (L.)Villars)

125. Kauri-thengia (Leea crispa D. Royen ex L.)

126. Beet (Beta vulgaris)

Appendix: X,n
150 plant species for cuisine of 101 herbs of Bohag Bihu

118. Halodhi (Curcuma longa L.)	119. Man dhoniya (Eryngium foetidum L.)	120. Dhekia (Diplazium escu lentum(Retz.)Sw.)
121. Ou tenga (Dillenia indica L.)	122. Nol tenga (Tetra stigma leucostaphylum)	123. Suka (Rumex acetosa)
124. Morolia (Stellaria media (L.)Villars)	125. Kauri-thengia (Leea crispa D. Royen ex L.)	126. Beet (Beta vulgaris)

Appendix: X,o
150 plant species for cuisine of 101 herbs of Bohag Bihu

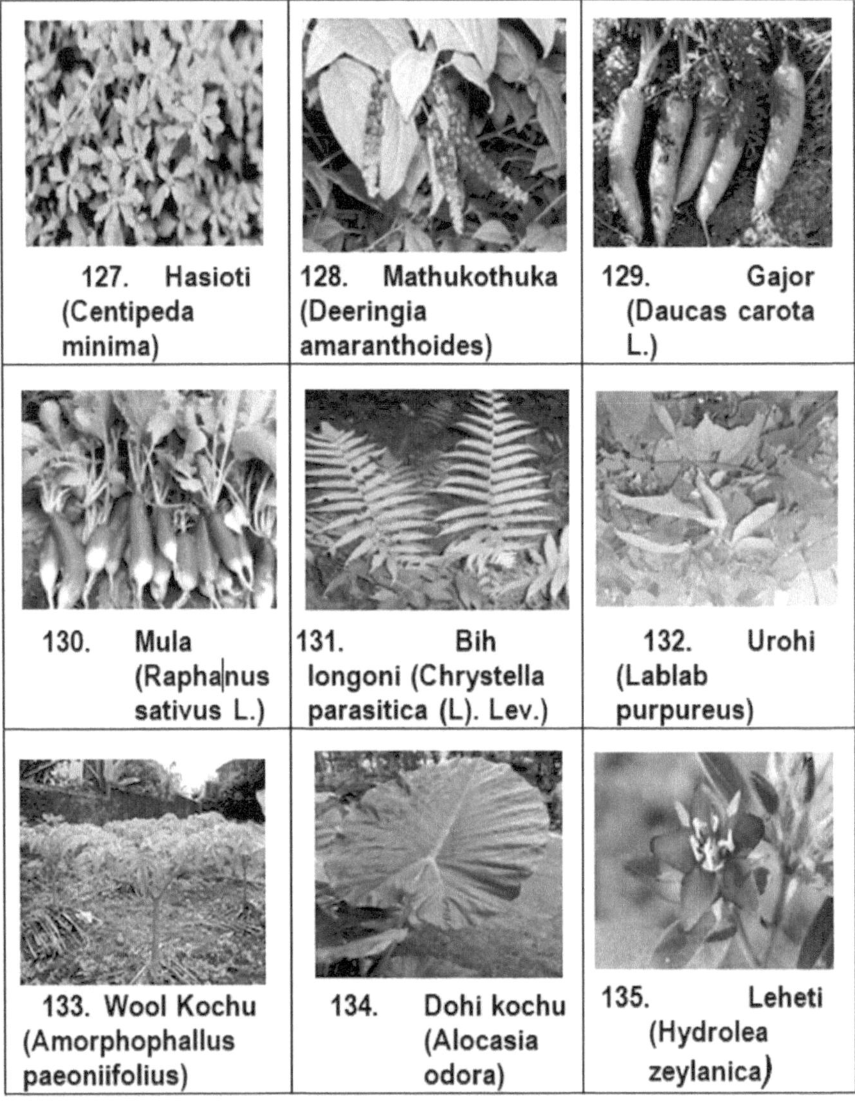

127. Hasioti (Centipeda minima)

128. Mathukothuka (Deeringia amaranthoides)

129. Gajor (Daucas carota L.)

130. Mula (Raphanus sativus L.)

131. Bih longoni (Chrystella parasitica (L). Lev.)

132. Urohi (Lablab purpureus)

133. Wool Kochu (Amorphophallus paeoniifolius)

134. Dohi kochu (Alocasia odora)

135. Leheti (Hydrolea zeylanica)

Appendix: X,p
150 plant species for cuisine of 101 herbs of Bohag Bihu

136. Edolia Kochu (Colocasia antiquorum)

137. Loborua (Codariocalyx motorius/ Desmodium gyrens)

138. Katari Dabua (Phas eolus lunatus)

139. Kon-Bilahi (Solanum pimpinellifolium)

140. Kotahi Bengena (Solanum ferox)

141. Khorua Bengena(Solanum melongena)

142. Bhimraj bon (Wedelia chinensis)

143. Bhomloti (Symplocos racemosa)

144. Kaath alu (Dioscorea bulbifera)

Appendix: X,q
150 plant species for cuisine of 101 herbs of Bohag Bihu

145. Bhat meteka (Mono choria vaginalis)	146. Titabahok (Justicia adhatoda syn Adatoda vasica)	147. Dubori bon (Cynodon dactylon)
148. Ban tioh (Cucumis maderaspatanus)	149. Bobosa bon (Elusine indica)	150. Moz (Albizzia lucica)

Sources of Appendix: X

The plant species were included in Appendix: X by consulting following sources, and images were taken from various websites.

1. Neog, Pradip (2008). Bihu Binandia. Jyoti Prakashan. pp. 58-59

2. Begum Sofika and Gogoi Rajib (2006). Herbal recipe prepared during Bohag or Rongali Bihu in Assam. Indian Journal of Traditional Knowledge : 6(3):2007 pp.417-422

3. Hussain Sadiqul (2018). 101 herbs and trees of Assam. https://youtu.be/xHz2RUJ3QJM

INDEX

9 781637 454930